Local Government Information and Training Needs in the 21st Century

Local Government Information and Training Needs in the 21st Century

Jack P. DeSario, Sue R. Faerman,
and
James D. Slack

QUORUM BOOKS
Westport, Connecticut • London

Library of Congress Cataloging-in-Publication Data

DeSario, Jack.
    Local government information and training needs in the 21st
century / Jack P. DeSario, Sue R. Faerman, and James D. Slack.
        p. cm.
    Includes bibliographical references and index.
    ISBN 0–89930–697–7
        1. Municipal government—Study and teaching—United States.
    2. Local government—Study and teaching—United States.
    3. Municipal officials and employees—Training of—United States.
    4. Local officials and employees—Training of—United States.
    I. Faerman, Sue R.   II. Slack, James D.   III. Title.
    JS49.D43   1994
    352'.0072'07073—dc20   93–30989

British Library Cataloguing in Publication Data is available.

Library of Congress Catalog Card Number: 93–30989
ISBN: 0–89930–697–7

First published in 1994

Quorum Books, 88 Post Road West, Westport, CT 06881
An imprint of Greenwood Publishing Group, Inc.

Printed in the United States of America

∞™

The paper used in this book complies with the
Permanent Paper Standard issued by the National
Information Standards Organization (Z39.48–1984).

10 9 8 7 6 5 4 3 2 1

Copyright Acknowledgments

We dedicate this book to our loved ones:

Mary Jo, Deanna, Nicole, and Paul DeSario;
and Paul and Adelaide DeSario

Barbara Fletcher, and Juhira and Ben LaNear;
and Miriam and Isidore Faerman

Janis, Sarah, and Samuel Slack;
and Rhoda and Michael Slack

Contents

Illustrations

FIGURE

Preface

We began writing this book during the Bush administration and finished it during the Clinton administration. While some dimensions of national politics have changed with the new president, one thing remains constant: New Federalism, as devised under the Carter and Reagan administrations, will continue to be the driving force in federal-local relations. Cities will have to continue to find creative ways in which to meet expanded responsibilities and unforeseen challenges. They will have to rely on resources that are increasingly independent of the federal government. This is especially true with Congress and the president searching for ways to cut the deficit and reduce the national debt.

Employee training and staff development represent one strategy for addressing the current and future challenges facing municipalities more effectively. They permit local governments to build a work force that is better trained, highly motivated, and more sensitive to both the expected processes and results of public service. Ultimately, training represents an investment in transforming the government employee into the public servant. Given the many potential avenues for acquiring training and assistance—private consultants, nonprofit organizations, in-house training programs, and university-based public sector outreach units—investments in this critical area can be comparatively inexpensive, and solutions can be found quite independent of federal government resources.

This book explores the training, education and assistance needs of municipalities as they prepare to enter the next century. We look at the current needs of city managers and mayors, as well as their anticipations of the future. In addition to their own perceived needs, other areas are explored in which we believe additional training and assistance are needed in order to gear up for the twenty-first century.

Sections of several publications are utilized in various parts of this book. Portions of James D. Slack's work, "Information Training and Assistance Needs of Municipal Governments" (*Public Administration Review* 50, no. 4, 1990, pp. 450–57), and portions of Slack's "Local Government Training and Education Needs for the Twenty-First Century" (*Public Productivity and Management Review* 13, no. 4, 1990, pp. 397–404), are used in Chapters 1 and 4. Portions of Slack's article, "The Public Administration of AIDS" (*Public Administration Review* 52, no. 1, 1992, pp. 77–80), and portions of Slack and Anelia Luna's "AIDS-Related Documents from 96 American Cities and Counties" (*Public Administration Review* 52, no. 3, 1992, pp. 305–9), are used in Chapters 2 and 5, respectively. Portions of the work of Jack P. DeSario et al., "Management of Human Resources in Local Government" (in Richard D. Bingham et al., *Managing Local Government: Public Administration in Practice*, Newbury Park, Calif.: Sage Publications, 1991), are used in Chapters 1 and 2. Finally, portions of Slack's book, *AIDS and the Public Work Force: Local Government Preparedness in Managing the Epidemic* (Tuscaloosa, Ala.: University of Alabama Press, 1991), are used in Chapter 2. The authors wish to extend thanks to the American Society for Public Administration, Sage Publications, Jossey-Bass, and the University of Alabama Press for permitting the use of these materials in this book.

We also wish to acknowledge assistance given by Frank McKenna, director of the Center for Governmental Research and Public Service at Bowling Green State University; Sylvester Murray, director of the Ohio Commission on the Public Service; and Scarlet Smith of the Carl Vinson Institute of Government at the University of Georgia. Each provided critical information about their respective organization's activities and uniformly did so either by fax or overnight express mail. We appreciate their quick responses to our questions about their organizations.

In addition, we wish to acknowledge assistance provided by several people at New Mexico State University. Professor Nancy Baker reviewed the final draft of the manuscript and did so critically, diligently, and swiftly—all characteristics greatly appreciated in good colleagues. Assistance with computer programming and statistical packages was provided by two very capable experts: Loretta Nash of the Computer and Networking Technologies Organization and Gloria Maese of the University Statistics Center. In addition, the following students in the MA in government program provided technical computer assistance: Gloria Friedman-Baron, Michael A. Gross, and Timothy J. Lamitie. Department of Government secretaries Stella Ramos and Ella Chavez helped immeasurably with the particulars of printing and copying the various drafts of the manuscript.

We also want to thank our editor at Quorum Books, Eric Valentine, for his encouragement, persistence, and patience throughout the process of writing this book. His support and advice were especially appreciated at the more trying times of completing this book.

Finally, we want to thank our loved ones for their understanding and encouragement throughout this process. Research and writing take up an incredible amount of time that could be invested in many other more pleasant activities. The fact that our loved ones understand this is only one of the reasons that they are very special people in our lives.

As in most scholarly pursuits, we truly benefitted from the help and kindness of many people. We alone, however, are responsible for all conceptual, methodological, and empirical errors and mistakes found within this book.

Local Government Information and Training Needs in the 21st Century

Chapter 1

Introduction to Local Government

Throughout this century, the American federal system of government has played an increasingly expanded role in providing and
regulating a vast array of domestic programs and policies. From
health care and housing to education and the environment,
expanded government responsibilities have led to a dramatic
growth in the size and capacity of federal and state bureaucracies.
Disparate strategies utilized in addressing domestic issues, from
Johnson's "Great Society" to Reagan's "New Federalism," have
also meant a substantial redefinition of the local government
function. Especially in the last decade or so, local government's
obligations to meet some of the most fundamental needs and
expectations of the citizenry have grown exponentially.

As in the case of federal and state bureaucracies, the ramifications of the increasingly complex and seemingly ever-changing role
played by local government require corresponding increments in
collective organizational capacity as well as individual employee
skills, motivation, and abilities. In essence, current and projected
challenges facing local government point toward the need for
greater levels of training and education for municipal employees.

Prior to a discussion about training needs, however, it is useful
to have a clearer picture of the nature of local government.
Acquiring this understanding is the purpose of this chapter.

OVERVIEW OF LOCAL GOVERNMENT

In terms of having a direct and immediate impact on the daily lives of the citizenry, there is no more important level of government than that of the municipality, county, and special local districts. As illustrated in Tables 1.1 and 1.2, municipalities dwarf state and federal governments both in terms of being the largest public employer and in terms of the sheer number of autonomous jurisdictions. As reported in Table 1.3, local governments spent over $450 billion in 1989—almost 30 percent of all public expenditures. Table 1.4 demonstrates that local governments play the most prominent role in delivering essential services such as education, health care, and public safety.

Local governments are generally classified by the Bureau of the Census into five major types—county, municipal, township, school district, and special district. County and local governments are organized and authorized in state constitutions and statutes, and they are established to provide general government: "In most states, the county functions as an administrative subdivision of the state. The county's responsibility is to carry out programs, such as highway maintenance or welfare services, that are estab-

Table 1.1
Government Employment by Type of Government, 1990

		Number of Employees (in millions)
Federal		3.1
State		4.5
Local		10.7
Counties	2.2	
Municipalities	2.6	
Townships	.4	
School Districts	4.9	
Special Districts	.6	
Total		**18.3**

Source: U.S. Bureau of the Census, Public Employment 1990, Series GE-90-1, p. VI.

Table 1.2
Number of Governmental Units

Federal	1
State	50
Counties	3,041
Cities	19,076
Townships	16,734
Special Districts	28,588
School Districts	14,851
Total	**82,341**

Source: U.S. Bureau of the Census, Public Employment
1990, Series GE-90-1, p. VI.

lished by the state" (Patterson, 1993:A–6). The county is generally governed by an elected group of county commissioners who possess both legislative and executive functions.

Table 1.3
Federal, State, and Local Direct General Expenditures and as a Percentage of All Expenditures, 1990

	Expenditures (in millions)		Percentage of Expenditures
Federal		855,234	50.8
State		333,256	19.7
Local		498,285	29.5
Municipalities	148,795		8.8
Counties	121,178		7.1
School Districts	176,547		10.5
Townships	17,545		1.1
Special Districts	34,220		2.0
Total		**1,686,775**	**100.0**
Federal Insurance Trust Expenditures	390,897		

Source: U.S. Advisory Commission on Intergovernmental Relations, Significant Features of
Fiscal Federalism, vol. 2, 1992, pp. 150-51.

Note: Direct general expenditures exclude intergovernmental expenditures and utility, liquor
store, and insurance trust expenditures. Federal insurance trust expenditures include
Social Security Old Age, Survivors, Disability, and Health Insurance, employer
retirement, railroad retirement, unemployment compensation, and veterans' life
insurance.

Table 1.4
Percentage of Direct Expenditures by Level of Government, 1990

	Federal	*State*	*Local*	*Total Spending* *(in millions)*
Education	8	21	71	298,185
Health and Hospitals	19	38	43	92,487
Police Protection	15	13	72	35,921

Source: U.S. Advisory Commission on Intergovernmental Relations, Significant Features of Fiscal Federalism, vol. 2, 1992, pp. 106-7, 146-47.

A municipal government is also authorized by state constitutions or statutes and provides general local government services for a specific population in a defined area. A municipality can be a city, village, borough, or town. Municipalities exist in part to implement the responsibilities of their state, but they also have direct and often independent responsibilities to residents within their jurisdictions. Municipal governments exercise primary responsibility for police and public safety, sanitation, water, and local transportation. Forms of municipal governance vary. "The traditional and most common form of municipal government is the mayor-council system, which includes the mayor as the chief executive and local council as the legislative body" (Patterson, 1993:A–6). Both the mayor and the council are popularly elected.

The major alternative form of municipal government is the council-manager system. This approach entrusts the executive function to a professionally trained, non-partisan manager who is hired and fired by the city council. This form of government is designed to insulate local decisions from political pressure while promoting expertise and objectivity.

Townships, unlike municipalities, are created to serve inhabitants of areas defined without regard to population concentration. This classification is applied to local governments in twenty states. School districts are generally governmental bodies that are fiscally and administratively independent of any other government and are responsible for the provision of local public education programs and policy. In most locations the chief executive for the schools is a superintendent who is hired by the locally elected school board. Special districts are local governmental units that are created to provide specific services that cannot be delivered by existing local government units or require the coordinated efforts of a number of governments. Special districts have limited authority and are not a general local government.

The role of municipalities is unique. In comparison with other local governmental units, it enjoys general governmental oversight and independent authority. Therefore, our analyses of the needs of local government officials will focus upon those involved in municipal governments.

CRISIS OF GOVERNING

Increased demands, dwindling financial support, technological advances, and demographic trends have placed a great deal of strain on public service delivery, public management, and public employees. Local governments have been particularly hard hit as a result of declines in local economic productivity and federal government cutbacks in assistance (Thai and Sullivan, 1989; Gold and Erickson, 1989). The declining economy and increased scarcity have led to diverse organizational responses. A number of private organizations have responded to the same national conditions by investing in training, informational, and developmental programs to enhance their competitiveness, expertise, and efficiency. The importance of employee training to private organizational success is best expressed by Robert Craig when he writes:

> Employee training and development (human resource development) has emerged as a major educational enterprise in the past three decades or so because of demand—demand in the workplace for employees at all levels, to improve performance in their present jobs, to acquire skills and knowledge to do new jobs, and to continue their career progress in a changing world of work. Employer organizations depend directly on the competence and productivity of their work forces for survival in the fierce competition of the world marketplace. Technological change, economic change, demographic change, and other forces continually create new needs for learning by the work force. (Craig, 1987:xiii)

Because many of the same issues of concern confront both the public and private sectors, the argument is easily made that public managers should match the employee training investments of their counterparts in business (Newell, 1989). In light of current constraints, however, it is important to ask why a public organization should commit to greater efforts in the areas of training and education. Part of the answer to this question is provided in definitions of training.

Blue Wooldridge has defined a training program as "an organized learning experience designed to enhance the ability of an employee to achieve a desired level of performance in a specific job. The ultimate objective of training is to improve organizational performance" (1988:205). The intent of most training and assistance programs is to aid government in "bringing about constructive change in the organization's current modus operandi" (Gabris, 1989:441) so that it can increase the level of productivity and thereby enhance its responsiveness to the needs and demands of the citizenry. Therefore, one reason to invest in training is that it is a method of enhancing by cost-effective means organizational productivity, effectiveness, and efficiency.

When reviewing financial commitments to training, the disparity between public and private organizations is significant. Some private organizations "spend as much as 15% of their payroll on these activities" (Wexley and Latham, 1991:4). Alternatively, studies have reported that "total expenditures on federal training are about $550 million . . . [or about] 0.8 percent of the amount spent on federal payroll. In contrast, one estimate for all Fortune 500 firms places training expenditures at 3.3 percent of the payroll" (Report of the National Commission on Public Service, 1989:193). These studies indicate that government spends about "three-quarters of 1 percent of its payroll dollars on civilian training, compared with 3 to 5 percent in the most effective private firms" (Report of the National Commission on Public Service, 1989:43).

Municipal governments exhibit a pattern of spending that is quite similar to that of their counterparts in federal agencies. A survey conducted by the International City Management Association (ICMA) of over thirteen hundred cities found that most units reported training budgets of less than one-half of 1 percent of the total municipal budget (Newell, 1989:311).

What makes these disparities between public and private sector organizations even more alarming is that governments have responded to current fiscal constraints, and the need for cutback management, by disproportionately cutting training budgets. A General Accounting Office (GAO) study of budget cuts, instituted in 1986 in response to mandates imposed by the Gramm-Rudman-Hollings deficit-control act, "found that 42 of 56 agencies reported training budget cuts. [Thirty] of these agencies reported reductions of 10% or more even though legal requirements required an average across-the-board reduction of only 4.3%" (Newell, 1989:15). Simply stated, training is usually the first area to be sacrificed when cuts are made in the public sector (Hyde and Shafritz, 1989).

In the case of municipalities, it seems that the desire among practitioners to explore additional managerial tools (Poister and Streib, 1989) is rising proportionately with the multitude of constraints that limit their capacity to expand the resources inside the managerial "tool kit" (Morgan, 1989). But unfortunately, the current era of cutback management has resulted in local government practitioners having to regard as luxury items the tools that may potentially increase organizational capacity.

Although there have not been many systematic evaluations of government training programs, the few that have been conducted have discovered significant benefits. A study by the U.S. Department of Education found "a four-to-one return-on-investment from every supervisory training dollar" (Newell, 1989:6). A study of excellence training among New York City municipal workers demonstrated improved productivity and organizational effectiveness (Timpone and Sussman, 1988).

Aside from the issues of increased productivity and efficiency, it is becoming apparent that public organizations are having difficulty attracting and retaining qualified employees. The Report of the National Commission on the Public Service notes with great concern that

> there is evidence on all sides of an erosion of performance and morale across government in America. Too many of our most talented public servants . . . are ready to leave. Too many of our brightest young people—those with the imagi-

nation and energy that are essential for the future—are unwilling to join. Meanwhile, the need for a strong public service is growing, not lessening.

The erosion in the attractiveness of public service at all levels . . . undermines the ability of government to respond effectively to the needs and aspirations of the American people, and ultimately damages the democratic process itself. (1989:IX and 1)

Two factors account for the public sector's difficulties in attracting and retaining qualified employees. First, changing demographic trends in our nation are having an important influence on age cohort, minority hiring, and women in the workplace. As Terry Newell has noted:

Since the mid-1960s the federal government has been able to attract high quality talent from a surplus of "baby boom" labor force entrants. The buyers market is over, at least until the year 2000. In fact, the national entry labor pool (workers aged 18–24) will drop by nearly 6 million people by 1994 from 1984 levels. (1989:16)

The impact of an aging population is particularly relevant to the public sector. Governments in face of competition are having difficulties in hiring the best and brightest of the new entrants into the work force. In addition, current government workers are typically older than the average age of those in the private economy (Hudson Institute, 1988:22). The aging of the public work force means more competition for promotions at a time when there are fewer job-advancement opportunities. Because public employees tend to be more highly educated, their skills are very desirable to prospective employers in the private sector. One additional problem for governments at all levels, therefore, is that private companies find public entities an attractive resource for securing skilled employees.

The lack of promotional opportunities and the marketability of top-level executives help explain why many leave public service for private-sector employment. According to the Merit System Protection Board, "40% of government executives left between

1979–1983, including 1,500 who resigned without retiring" (Newell, 1989:18).

An analysis of employees who left government employment highlights the second major explanation for the public sector's difficulties in attracting and retaining qualified employees—inadequate compensation. Almost 40 percent of the senior federal executives who left government service in 1985 cited inadequate compensation as an important consideration in making their decision to leave (Report of the National Commission on Public Service, 1989:34).

There are an abundance of statistics that document significant growing pay differentials between the public and private sector. The salary gap between senior executives in government and the private sector was 65 percent in 1987 and, we estimate, will be nearly 100 percent by the turn of the century. Furthermore, the National Commission on Public Service notes that the

> average starting salary for careers in private sector consulting and research has gone up 15% in real terms over the past decade, while pay for careers in banking, finance and insurance has jumped 18%. During the same period, the real average starting salary for a career in the federal government has fallen 20 percent and now trails the private sector on average by about $6,000. (Report of the National Commission on Public Service, 1989:24)

This problem is even more acute for local government and municipal employees because their average earnings tend to be lower than those of federal and state employees (U.S. Bureau of Census, 1990).

Together the problems of morale, advancement, and salary differentials have created an environment that is not attractive to new employees and has motivated current employees to seek alternative careers. These factors explain why the National Commission on Public Service found that only 13 percent of senior executives would recommend that young people start their careers in government. Furthermore, this negative perception of government employment seems to be reflected in the opinions of young, talented, prospective employees. For instance, a survey of 865 honor students from four-year colleges found that only "6% felt that government work was challenging and intellectually stimulating" (Report of the National Commission on Public Service, 1989:179). In fact, state-local employment was rated next to last (above only military service) in comparison with other employment options for a number of considerations, including challenging work, opportunity for personal growth, pleasant conditions, and financial rewards.

Many analysts agree that government organizations are showing the signs of distress and decay from lack of public commitment and investment. As one observer notes, government programs, employees, and managers "have been undervalued for at least a decade now" (Glenn-Ryan and Guss, 1989:187). The erosion of government performance is exhibited by low morale and the declining skills of the public work force. Various measures of skill levels, including PACE and SAT scores, indicate that the abilities of new hires are on the decline (Hudson Institute, 1988).

These realities provide another compelling rationale for public training. Public training, aside from its ability to improve effectiveness or efficiency, has also been found to "enhance worker job satisfaction and morale" (Haas, 1991:226). Only by improving working conditions and worker satisfaction will the public sector be able to retain and attract quality employees.

These problems are clearly having an impact upon local government managers. A survey of local government officials asked them to indicate their "most pressing, troublesome or urgent internal management challenge or problem." Two of the most important issues identified were: providing more staff with diverse expertise, education, experience, values, orientations, and expectations; and providing for staff and employee development (Zar and Stephon, 1991:14). Almost all of the respondents identified education and training as important to the effective performance of their work.

As critical as training and education are now to the public sector, their role will continue to grow in the future. Demographic trends will have a bearing on the enhanced importance of training and education. Projections by the Committee on Economic Development and others indicate that in the year 2000, 85% of the recruitment pool will be composed of women, minorities, and recent immigrants. For the managers of the future, the task will be not only ensuring diversity by recruiting; it will be to guarantee to a newly diverse work force adequate management training and development opportunities. (Report of the National Commission on Public Service, 1989:152)

Given the economic restraints imposed upon the public sector, it is clear that local governments will not be able to hire the high skill levels and expertise they require. Rather, the most practical strategy for governments to pursue these talents is to develop the skills they need within their work force. The realities of the twenty-first century have prompted the National Commission on Public Service to conclude that "training must receive a higher priority in coming years both to ensure that talented public servants are allowed to grow and to address the changing public agenda" (1989:43).

ORGANIZATION OF THIS BOOK

It is with an eye toward the twenty-first century that this book examines the training and assistance needs of municipalities. This introductory chapter has attempted to provide a general understanding of the nature and context of local government. The second chapter provides a more detailed analysis of the changing fiscal, legal, and social environment within which municipalities operate. Chapter 3 presents training theories and approaches that will help local-government practitioners prepare to face the challenges of the twenty-first century. Chapters 4 and 5 look at current and future training needs of city managers and mayors across the United States. Chapter 6 summarizes the book's arguments and findings and offers some suggestions about what must be done to increase the role of education and training within municipal government.

Chapter 2

The Changing Environment of Local Government

The issues that local governments will be required to address during the twenty-first century promise to be significantly different from those of the past. To prepare for these challenges, the public sector must attempt to identify the important features of this changing environment. This chapter focuses on four of the most important trends that must be systematically evaluated: New Federalism, legal issues in the public workplace, evolving collective-bargaining requirements, and health issues—especially those pertaining to the Acquired Immunodeficiency Syndrome (AIDS) epidemic.

NEW FEDERALISM

Changing relationships among national, state, and local government have been characterized by many analysts as the New Federalism (Elazar, 1984). This term has been utilized to emphasize the shifts in responsibility and funding for many domestic programs. No unit of government has been more profoundly affected by New Federalism than local governments. Over the past decade local governments have assumed a great deal more of the responsibility for public-sector service delivery and regulation. Accompanying these increased burdens have been dramatic changes in the fiscal relationship among national, state, and local governments. Paradoxically, as local governments have assumed greater responsibility, the growth in financial aid provided by the other governments has declined.

While a new Democratic administration has been elected, we feel that President Clinton's philosophy toward federalism does not differ extensively from that of his immediate predecessors. Even if his personal views about federalism were dramatically different, both moderate and conservative forces currently controlling the Democratic Party would prevent major deviations from the past twelve years of Republican rule. In essence, the dynamics of New Federalism will continue to underscore the importance of understanding the changing role of local government in the public sector.

The national government, confronted with budgetary problems during the 1980s, enacted a number of laws and administrative mandates that required state and local governments to assume additional regulatory and financial responsibility in the areas of education, environment, labor management, housing, and transportation. It has been estimated that these federal mandates cost state and local governments "$100 billion a year" (Berman, 1992:51). State governments responded to these shifting obligations by passing their own laws and mandates and further delegating responsibilities for a number of domestic issues to local governments. As Berman notes: "The estimated number of mandates varies widely from state to state. In Virginia, statutory and regulatory mandates run into the thousands. South Carolina has some 500 mandates, while Maryland has more than twice this number" (1992:52).

These mandates, similar to their federal counterparts, required localities to accept increased domestic responsibilities while also bearing the costs of these programs.

The legal relationship among local, state, and national government leaves the local government with few options but to respond to these mandates. When reviewing the interaction between the national and local government, it is clear that the national government possesses important legal and economic powers.

The national government can issue direct orders to local governments with which compliance is mandatory. Direct orders derive their authority from the U.S. Constitution and the supremacy clause. In other words, the Constitution specifies functions over which the national government is supreme. Pursuant to these constitutional prerogatives, the national government can not only require conformity but can also preempt any actions to the contrary that are taken by state or local governments. This power has been exercised for issues such as employment, environment, commerce, and education policy.

Garcia v. San Antonio Metropolitan Transit Authority illustrates the pervasiveness of federal powers. The U.S. Supreme Court held in this case that the Federal Fair Labor Standards Act was binding upon municipal governments in regard to the salaries and overtime payments they could offer their employees. As a result of this decision, many observers wonder whether any function of local government is beyond federal reach. Aside from the important power implications of this decision, it is important to note that compliance costs with this one act alone were "variously estimated at $2–4 billion" (Wright, 1988:43).

Even in areas where the federal government does not have constitutional authority, it can use its financial powers to gain compliance from states and localities. This approach is usually referred to as a crossover sanction. A crossover sanction occurs when "a recipient's failure to comply with regulations in one program can result in the termination (or reduction) of funds available in a separately authorized program" (Wright, 1988:369).

The legal relationship between state and local governments has also been well defined by the courts. Historically, the courts have concluded that local governments are merely political subdivisions of the state. Therefore, it has been consistently held that local governments may only exercise those powers specifically granted to them by the state. In practice, it has been found that "the amount of discretion varies by region, type of local government, and type of function performed. Units in some parts of the country enjoy more discretion than in others" (Berman, 1992:52). However, after noting this variation it must be emphasized that the discretion provided relates generally to the structure and organization of local government, rather than to the actual functions they perform or how they may raise and spend revenue.

By virtue of their status as the "low person" of legal federalism, it is not easy for local governments to circumvent the mandates of state and national government. This realization makes it essential to understand the changing patterns of fiscal federalism that have accompanied the delegation of many of these programs.

Table 2.1 indicates that during the 1980s the national government spent a smaller percentage of all direct public expenditures, while the role of local government increased. This reflects the delegation of programs that occurred over the decade. With the increase of responsibility assumed by local government, intergovernmental grants-in-aid take on even greater importance. Grants-in-aid are important because many

> state and local governments have weaker economic bases and less productive systems of taxation than the national government possesses, yet the former provide the great bulk of public services in health, education, welfare, housing, highway construction, police protection, parks and recreation, conservation, and agricultural services. (Gordon, 1992:85)

Table 2.2 demonstrates that while the national government has shifted programs to the states and localities, it has not provided them with the additional financing needed. In fact, from 1980 to 1982 there was an aggregate cut in federal grants-in-aid. The proportion of state and local government outlays from federal sources has decreased since 1980. In terms of constant dollars, the federal government provided the states and localities with less revenue in 1991 ($129 billion) than in 1980 ($127.6 billion).

Table 2.1
Federal, State, and Local Direct General Expenditures, 1985 and 1990

	1985		1990	
	Expenditures (in billions)	*Percentage of Expenditures*	*Expenditures (in billions)*	*Percentage of Expenditures*
Federal	$640	54	$855	51
State	$223	18	$333	20
Local	$329	28	$498	30

Source: U.S. Advisory Commission on Intergovernmental Relations, <u>Significant Features of Fiscal Federalism</u>. vol. 2, 1992, pp. 150-51.

Table 2.2
Federal Grants-in-Aid, Selected Years

	Amount (in billions)	Percentage of Total State-Local Outlay	Constant Dollars (in 1987 dollars)
1980	91.5	26	127.6
1982	88.2	22	106.5
1985	105.9	21	113.0
1987	108.4	18	108.4
1989	122.0	17	112.0
1991	152.0	21	129.0

Source: U.S. Advisory Commission on Intergovernmental Relations, Significant Features of Fiscal Federalism, vol. 2, 1992, p. 60.

The impact of federal retrenchment in grants-in-aid can be seen in Table 2.3. From 1980 to 1989 the federal contribution to local government revenue declined from 8 percent to 3 percent of all local revenue. Predictably, the "own source" revenue of local governments increased during this period from 60 percent to 67 percent. These figures, while demonstrating the increased financial burdens of the localities, probably underestimate the economic hardships.

A report by the National League of Cities revealed that

for fiscal year 1991 approximately 60.9% of all cities expected that general fund expenditures would exceed general fund revenues, and although large cities (73.5%) were more likely to predict a general fund deficit, medium-size and small

Table 2.3
Local Grant Revenues by Source for Selected Years

	Total (billions)	Own Source (billions)	% of total	Federal Grants (billions)	% of total	State Grants (billions)	% of total
1980	$258	$156	60	$21	8	$ 81	31
1985	$402	$264	66	$22	5	$116	29
1989	$532	$357	67	$18	3	$158	30

Source: U.S. Advisory Commission on Intergovernmental Relations, Significant Features of Fiscal Federalism, vol. 2, 1992, p. 78.

cities were not immune to deficits either. [Over half of these cities expected deficits in their general fund.] Despite this reality, many cities will indeed balance their budgets, but there will be a major price to pay. Since cities cannot borrow to finance operating deficits, the price will be cutbacks in city services and deferral of maintenance. (Pammer, 1992:6)

In addition to these actions many governments are raising eligibility requirements for their programs, collecting charges for their services, increasing taxes, and privatizing services. Many of these strategies simply mean fewer services for fewer people.

The financial response of local government to cuts in intergovernmental revenue is presented in Table 2.4. Local governments have replaced declining grants-in-aid with an increase in property, sales, and other taxes. However, the single largest increase has been in the charges and miscellaneous category.

New Federalism has meant more responsibility and less financial assistance for local government. Localities will have to develop strategies for responding to this environment while maintaining essential services and programs. Local officials have already had some success in passing legislation that would allow them to levy new taxes and fees: "Currently, 28 states allow local governments the option of levying a local sales tax" (Berman, 1992:54). Some localities are also utilizing impact fees that they can impose on developers to help cover the costs of development. For example, localities can charge for the expense of providing roads, sewers, and water to new projects.

Table 2.4
Local General Revenue by Source for Selected Years, Percentage of Total

	Inter-governmental	Total Local	Property Tax	Income Tax	Sales Tax	Other	Charges and Miscellaneous
1980	44	56	28	2	5	1.6	19
1985	39	61	28	2	6	1.6	23
1989	37	63	29	2	6	2.3	23
1990	37	63	29	2	6	2.1	24

Source: U.S. Advisory Commission on Intergovernmental Relations, Significant Features of Fiscal Federalism, vol. 2, 1992, p. 119.

It has been found that local governments are viewed more favorably by citizens than are federal or state governments (Berman, 1992). From a political perspective, municipal officials must rely on these public perceptions to implement effective management programs and financial strategies to address the changing environment. Self-reliance will be an important concept for localities in the twenty-first century. Local government will have to take the initiative in pioneering new innovations that can help them achieve their goals.

LEGAL ISSUES AND PUBLIC WORKPLACE COMPLIANCE

Public personnel policies determine who is hired, promoted, and fired. Anti-discrimination and affirmative action laws of the past few decades have had a profound impact upon hiring procedures, employment practices, and ultimately, the demographic composition of local governments. These policies and their underlying logic are among the most controversial and complex developments that the public sector must confront. In addressing concerns about workplace diversity, it is essential to understand the social implications and legal requirements surrounding this issue.

As mentioned previously, local government is the largest focal point of public-sector employment, accounting for approximately 58 percent of all of the government work force. The local government work force has expanded by more than 40 percent since 1970 and in many communities it is the largest single employer (DeSario et al., 1991:77). The magnitude and nature of local government employment make it important to understand current personnel policies.

Diversity in the workplace has become a central concern for public personnel managers. Municipalities are being urged to address the diversity issue for a number of considerations. First, the national government has required the vigorous enforcement of the legal guarantees of equal protection and due process. These rights have been expanded significantly to state and local governments. Second, the inclusion of women, minorities, and the disabled in the public-sector work force will result in "passive representation" and will therefore enhance the equity, efficiency and effectiveness of government programs (Mosher, 1968). Finally, as noted by the Report of the National Commission on Public Service, by the "year 2000, 85% of the recruitment pool will be composed of women, minorities, and recent immigrants" (1989:152). Therefore, public personnel policies must be prepared for, and take advantage of, the changing characteristics of public employees.

Legal mandates related to the issue of diversity focus on two major strategies: equal employment opportunity (EEO) law and affirmative action (AA) policies. Equal employment opportunity forbids employers from discriminating in their hiring and firing decisions on the basis of sex, race, ethnicity, or disability. Affirmative action encourages special consideration for targeted groups that have been the victims of past discrimination. "Collectively, these policies seek to eliminate all discriminatory actions in personnel administration and to remedy the effects of past discrimination as well. Executives and administrators in business and government make EEO/AA regulations and decisions primarily on the authority of laws passed by Congress" (Blease Graham, Jr., 1990:177).

To understand the basic guidelines with which the public sector must comply, it is essential to review and interpret significant civil rights statutes and cases. The Civil Rights Act of 1964 was the first major legislative effort to prohibit workplace discrimination on the basis of an individual's race, color, religion, sex, or national origin. Title VII of the Civil Rights Act specifically addressed workplace discrimination and made it illegal for a private-sector employer to discriminate in any employment practice, including hiring, promotion, and firing.

However, it was not until the passage of the Equal Employment Opportunity Act (EEOA) of 1972, which amended the Civil Rights Act, that state and local government employment practices were specifically regulated. Aside from prohibiting public-sector workplace discrimination, EEOA also required states and localities to develop affirmative action plans to address minority hiring practices. As a result, municipalities had an affirmative obligation to recruit minority groups such as women and African-Americans.

Pursuant to these enactments, the federal government established the Equal Employment Opportunity Commission (EEOC) to receive and investigate job discrimination complaints. The EEOC has the authority, if the charges are accurate, to attempt to negotiate an agreement and remedy. If a voluntary agreement cannot be reached, the EEOC may take its action to the federal courts. The power of the EEOC to independently litigate civil actions for workplace discrimination is very important because many of the victims of discrimination lack the financial resources to pursue their claims.

The Equal Pay Act of 1963 requires that all public- and private-sector employers provide equal pay for equal work. This legislation specifically eliminates wage differentials between men and women in an effort to address sex discrimination.

The Vocational Rehabilitation Act of 1973 prohibits public and private organizations from discriminating against disabled workers who are otherwise qualified. Section 504 of the Act provides a very broad definition of "handicap." A person can qualify as handicapped in three ways: by having a mental or physical impairment that limits participation in one of life's major activities; by having a record of having had a mental or physical impairment that limits participation in one of life's major activities; or by being regarded as having a mental or physical condition that limits participation in one of life's major activities.

The 1990 Americans with Disabilities Act (ADA) uses the same three-pronged definition of "disabled," the contemporary term for persons with mental or physical impairments. It also strengthens the rights of disabled workers by calling for reasonable accommodation, limiting the use of pre-employment medical examinations, and requiring employment discrimination against the disabled to fall within the investigative jurisdiction of the EEOC. The broad scope of the Rehabilitation Act and the ADA is attested to by the fact that they apply to workers with alcoholism, drug addiction, and the human immunodeficiency virus (HIV).

In interpreting these statutory provisions, federal courts have developed important distinctions and requirements that are of direct relevance to the actions of public sector managers. Pursuant to the Constitution and statutory law, the Supreme Court has prohibited all intentionally discriminatory employment practices and has encouraged an environment of equal opportunity. The Court has stated that in most workplace settings, it need only order the employer or union to cease discriminatory practices to achieve its legal objectives. However, the Court has also recognized that to achieve equal opportunity, it may be necessary in some circumstances to require "the employer or union to take affirmative steps to end discrimination and effectively to enforce Title VII" (*Local 28 of the Sheetmetal Workers International Association v. EEOC*, 478 U.S. 421, 1986).

It is in this area of affirmative action that our judicial system has developed a complex and controversial set of standards that govern the public workplace. One important consideration that the court has utilized in designing the appropriate legal remedy for the workplace is whether or not an employer has a history of past discrimination. A finding of past discrimination in the work force can lead to the application of stringent affirmative action requirements, including quotas.

For example, in *U.S. v. Paradise*, the Supreme Court upheld a court order that required the state of Alabama to allocate half of its state trooper promotions to qualified black candidates. The apparent severity of this decision must be considered in the context of the court's findings that none of Alabama's 232 state troopers with a rank of corporal or higher was black and that Alabama had a history of past discrimination. These considerations led the court to state that, as a result of its determinations, any charges of reverse discrimination were not valid because the equal protection rights of other workers is not violated when a quota advances "a compelling governmental interest in remedying past and present discrimination" (*U.S. v. Paradise*, 480 U.S. 149, 1987).

In *Local 28 of the Sheetmetal Workers International Association v. EEOC*, the Supreme Court explained its considerable authority under Title VII. The Court stated that affirmative race-conscious relief is an appropriate remedy for past discrimination. The justices reasoned that race-conscious affirmative relief furthers the broad purposes underlying the statute:

Title VII was designed to achieve equality of employment opportunities and remove barriers that have operated in the past to favor an identifiable group of white employees over other employees. . . . In order to foster equal employment opportunities, Congress gave the lower courts broad power

under 706 (G) to fashion "the most complete relief possible"
to remedy past discrimination. (*Local 28 of the Sheetmetal
Workers International v. EEOC*, 478 U.S. 421, 1986)

It is this logic that the Court utilized to reconcile the obvious
tensions between equal employment and affirmative action. In
this case, the Supreme Court stated that for most cases of employment discrimination, the Court will only have to order the
employer to cease discriminatory practices in order to achieve
equal opportunity. However, even with this caveat, the Court
went on to identify an important role for affirmative action not
only for recalcitrant employers but also in some circumstances
where an employer formally ceases to engage in discriminatory
practices. The Court reasoned that even when an employer aban-
dons formal discriminatory practices, informal mechanisms such
as the employer's reputation may operate to discourage minority
employment. The Court concluded that in "these circumstances,
affirmative race-conscious relief may be the only means available
to assure equality of employment opportunities and to eliminate
those discriminatory practices and devices which have fostered
racially stratified job environments to the disadvantage of minority citizens" (*Local 28 of the Sheetmetal Workers International Association v. EEOC*, 478 U.S. 421, 1986). In this case the Supreme Court
held that Title VII does not prohibit a court from ordering relief to
individuals who are not victims.

The absence of a history of discrimination leads to modified
judicial strategies for promoting workplace diversity. The often-
quoted case of the *Regents of the University of California v. Bakke*
forced the Supreme Court to determine whether an educational
institution that did not have a history of past discrimination could
establish quotas for the preferential admission of minority students. The Court concluded that Allan Bakke, a white student
who felt he had been denied admission although more qualified
than black students admitted under the quota system, had to be
admitted and that, in the context of this case, the quota system
developed by the University of California at Davis medical school
was unconstitutional.

When interpreting the policy implications of *Bakke* it must be
recognized that this decision contained six different opinions,

with none receiving majority support. It is also important to ensure that the results of this case are not applied too generally but rather within the narrow confines for which it was intended. For example, while the plurality opinion concluded that the quota system instituted in these circumstances (no history of discrimination) was too rigid, it also conceded that race could be considered even as a factor in admissions policy. Affirmative action was not being discarded; it could be applied in a different form even in a setting devoid of past discrimination.

The case of *Johnson v. Transportation Agency, Santa Clara County* affirms this interpretation. Pertinent to the outcome of this case is a clause in the EEOA that requires all local governments with fifteen or more employees to adopt an affirmative action plan. Local governments are required to report annually to the EEOC on the progress that they have made in increasing minority employment.

Pursuant to these requirements, Santa Clara County developed an affirmative action plan that stipulated that the sex or race of a qualified candidate could be considered when promoting employees to positions with traditionally segregated job classifications. Subsequently, when there was an opening for a road dispatcher, a number of individuals applied, and nine were deemed qualified. In accordance with its plan, Santa Clara promoted Diane Joyce, who was ranked fourth, over Paul Johnson, who was ranked second. Johnson's claims of reverse discrimination and equal rights violation were dismissed by the Court. In recognition of the requirements and objectives of the EEOA, the Supreme Court held that the agency

> appropriately took into account as one factor the sex of Diane Joyce in determining she should be promoted to the road dispatcher position. The decision to do so was made pursuant to an affirmative action plan that represents a moderate, flexible, case-by-case approach to effecting a gradual improvement in the representation of minorities and women in the agency's work force. Such a plan is fully consistent with Title VII, for it embodies the contribution that voluntary employer action can make in eliminating the vestiges of discrimination in the work-place. (*Johnson v. Transportation Agency, Santa Clara County* 480 vs 616, 1987)

This decision is significant because it upheld the legality of affirmative action plans that allow a public employer to consider race and gender when addressing underrepresentation without having to admit to or have a history of past discrimination. Employees who don't receive promotions in accord with these plans are devoid of a legal remedy.

Another important consideration that the courts apply to public-sector employment practices is whether the policy has a discriminatory intent, as opposed to a disproportionate impact. Policies motivated by discriminatory intent are illegal per se. Employment practices that have a disproportionate impact are more difficult to evaluate. The Supreme Court has maintained that disproportionate impact alone does not warrant a conclusion of purposeful and unlawful discrimination. However, the courts have also invalidated personnel practices, procedures, and tests that, although neutral on their face and even neutral in intent, were found to freeze the status quo of prior discriminatory practices (Carper et al., 1991).

In the case of *Griggs v. Duke Power*, all employees of a company were required to have a high school diploma to be eligible for promotions. Although this requirement applied to all workers, it was found to have a disproportionate impact upon black employees. White males in this region had a high school graduation rate over two times greater than that of black males. After considering these facts, the Supreme Court held that any organization that institutes personnel requirements resulting in a disproportionate impact must demonstrate that these employment standards are job-related. Absent evidence that requirements are job-related, they will be held illegal. This decision has been relied upon to invalidate a number of civil service tests, height and weight specifications, and experience requirements that have operated to the detriment of women and ethnic minorities.

Local government enthusiasm for and compliance with equal employment and affirmative action directives varies greatly among municipalities. One survey of municipal personnel administrators found that larger urban governments were more likely to express support for affirmative action than those in smaller cities (Davis and West, 1984). Even among supporters, however, the ideal of promoting workplace diversity does not correspond with efforts to accomplish this objective. Another survey of municipalities with populations over 100,000 discovered that these local governments still depend upon "traditional selection and hiring methods; over 95 percent use a written test for at least one job and about one-third of cities have actually expanded use of written tests" (Blease Graham, Jr., 1990:189). Slack and Sigelman's survey of 280 city managers found that while managers claim to support affirmative action, they "balk at the specific policies and procedures designed to implement these general principles" (1987:678). Most city managers opposed the involvement of minority leaders in city recruitment and promotion procedures or the development of hiring targets or timetables. In fact, despite Supreme Court rulings that the race and gender of qualified candidates may be considered, most city managers still prefer traditional merit-system hiring practices.

Public sector statistics indicate that minority employment has been rising steadily over the last decade for all levels of government. At the federal level, 1987 figures indicate that blacks accounted for "16.8 percent of the [entire] work force, far above their 11 percent share of the national workforce. Hispanics by contrast, were 6.6 percent of the nation's employees, but only 5.1 percent of Federal workers" (Hudson Institute, 1988:23). Women make up about 40 percent of the federal workplace, as compared with 44 percent of the total work force. Despite these encouraging trends, minority groups remain disproportionately employed in the lowest-paying and least-skilled jobs. For example, in the highest federal ranks, GS 13–15, blacks account for 5.5 percent, Hispanics 2.2 percent, and women 12.4 percent of the total.

At the state and local levels, a national survey conducted by EEOC found that these governments have done a better job of incorporating blacks, women, and other ethnic minorities into the work force (Dometrius and Sigelman, 1984). "From 1979 to 1990, the number of female and minority municipal heads (including majors and chief appointed administrative officers) have increased from 4.5% to 11.6% and 1.8% to 5.6% respectively" (DeSario et al., 1991:91–92).

While statistical gains are encouraging, many substantive concerns regarding the accommodation of workplace diversity remain and may even be increasing. A survey of state government employees in five states found that about 20 percent of state employees perceive some form of job discrimination (Blease Graham, Jr., 1990:188). A study of sexual harassment conducted by the U.S. Merit Systems Protection Board (MSPB) estimated that sexual harassment alone "cost the federal government $267 million over two years in lost productivity and employee turnover. . . . It also reduces productivity and poses serious legal problems" (Neugarten, 1990:205). The MSPB also found that 42 percent of women surveyed reported being sexually harassed. Neugarten cites a *U.S. News and World Report* article indicating that "formal complaints [of sexual harassment] filed with the EEOC rose from 4,272 in 1981 to 7,273 in 1985" (1990:207). While many would like to believe that it is the reporting of the problems that has increased and not the extent of the problem, it is also possible that the public sector is having major difficulties in managing greater workplace diversity.

In preparing municipal governments for the twenty-first century, local government must develop strategies to accommodate and promote workplace diversity. Local public managers must develop appropriate affirmative action plans, workplace policy statements, and skill-training programs to attract and retain minority employees. Once minorities are attracted, their special needs must also be accommodated. Employee surveys, education programs, cultural awareness training can all be utilized to facilitate a harmonious workplace.

Some local governments have taken positive steps toward addressing the issue of diversity in the workplace. A 1992 Public Personnel Survey conducted by the International Personnel Management Association found that 20 percent of the respondents indicated that they have implemented a cultural diversity program. Another encouraging sign is that this survey indicated that the number of agencies offering a child care center nearly doubled, from 5 percent in 1990 to 9 percent in 1992.

PUBLIC-SECTOR COLLECTIVE BARGAINING

One of the most important developments in public personnel management at the state and local levels has been the introduction and evolution of public-sector collective bargaining. Collective bargaining in the public sector refers to the legal obligation of management and employee representatives to enter into a bilateral determination of the wages and conditions of employment. Collective bargaining laws have established new legal relationships and personnel administration processes that students and practitioners of local government need to understand. New administrative entities—state employee administration boards, arbitrators, and fact finders—are now essential elements of local public personnel administration.

To comprehend the true political and administrative significance of recent collective bargaining developments in the public sector, it is important to review traditional approaches of local governments to personnel administration. Prior to the 1960s, public employees had a limited role in determining their wages and working conditions. Traditionally, mayors, the civil service, and councils were vested with the unilateral authority to determine public-sector workplace conditions, rules, and wages. This approach to public employment was based upon the logic of the sovereignty doctrine. The sovereignty doctrine maintains that federal, state, and local governments represent the sovereign power of the people. In accord with this doctrine, any delegation of decision-making power to employees, which would provide them a voice in the determination of the terms and conditions of their public employment, is inconsistent with public sovereignty and the principles of public accountability.

Until recently, state and local governments have used this perspective to unilaterally determine public-sector work conditions. Attempts by unions to gain representative and collective bargaining rights were viewed as illegal encroachments upon the authority of government.

The sovereignty argument became increasingly difficult for public managers to advance as governments at all levels delegated significant policy-making authority to public bureaucracies and the private sector. The courts even affirmed the legality of these actions. In 1962 President John Kennedy issued Executive Order 10988, which recognized for the first time the legitimacy of collective bargaining for most federal employees. In addition, local governments such as those in Philadelphia, Cincinnati, and New York provided their employees with some limited collective bargaining rights.

These developments led to a change in the philosophy of public-sector management from unilateral denial of collective bargaining to establishing public employee participation in a manner consistent with the requirements of democracy. By the 1960s, the benefits of collective bargaining to the public sector were being widely extolled. It was argued that collective bargaining would enhance employee performance, productivity, responsiveness, and innovation.

Since the early 1960s, the public sector has experienced a large increase in union membership. In 1962 about 1.6 million state and local government employees belonged to a union; by 1987 this figure had grown to 4.9 million. At the local level, approximately 47 percent of all employees are members of a union, while 51 percent of all municipal workers are unionized (Gordon, 1992:313).

The scope and process of local government collective bargaining is dictated by state statute. Currently, there are more than 100 laws outlining labor relations in the fifty states.

State legislation varies in scope and administration. Some states have a single comprehensive statute covering all public employees. Other states have numerous statutes, each covering a particular type of employee (teachers, police, municipal or state workers) or specific regions or counties of the state. States having numerous statutes may permit collective bargaining for some public employees but not others. Some states still prohibit collective bargaining. The types of issues over which unions may bargain and how they bargain also vary significantly from state to state. To provide a general oversight of collective bargaining in states and localities, it is important to identify their essential components. The major components of collective bargaining are the right to bargain, the scope of bargaining, impasse resolution procedures, union security, and strike provisions.

The right to bargain can range from a prohibition of collective bargaining to "meet and confer" laws, to the provision of comprehensive collective bargaining. Meet and confer laws only require public employers to consent to discussions about working conditions with their employees. However, public entities are neither bound to enter into written agreements nor to abide by them if they do.

Among states that have enacted collective bargaining laws—and the great majority have—their administration varies. The scope of bargaining in a state is generally broken into three categories: mandatory, permissive, and prohibited topics for collective bargaining. Mandatory issues are those that management must negotiate with an employee organization, while permissive issues may be negotiated at the discretion of management. Prohibited topics are the exclusive domain of managers and are often referred to as "management rights." Most states follow the terms of the National Labor Relations Act and define the scope of bargaining as wages, hours, and terms and conditions of employment.

During the course of bargaining over mandatory or permissive issues, an impasse between management and employees may occur. The approach that a state statute dictates at this juncture is particularly important. Some states provide for voluntary binding arbitration, while others have compulsory binding arbitration laws. By 1986, almost half of the states had compulsory arbitration in some form.

Impasse resolution procedures may vary to include mediation, fact finding, arbitration, or a combination of these procedures. Mediation is generally an informal process in which a mediator attempts to promote voluntary settlements. Fact finding, which is often required in a state only after mediation fails, is a more formal process. Fact finding generally imposes formal procedures and rules of presentation and evidence. Management and employee representatives are required to collect and present data relative to the disputed issues between them. Based upon this information, the fact finder will issue a written report for settlement, which in most states is non-binding. Arbitrations are conducted in much the same manner as fact finding except that the arbitrator's report is final and binding. Although provisions often are made for appeal of the arbitrator's report to a state employee relations board or state courts, the findings are generally upheld unless they are clearly unreasonable.

While compulsory binding arbitration provides an alternative to public employee strikes, it has significant political ramifications. Mandatory arbitration restructures traditional governmental relationships by limiting public management authority, eliminating employer unilateralism, and transforming the administration of our political democracy. Arbitration procedures entrust non-elected arbitrators with the authority to make binding decisions that determine personnel costs of governments, the amount of taxes a government must impose, and the basic working relationship between public employees and managers. Arbitrators are generally selected from regional or state arbitration societies and tend to be disinterested lawyers and professors. Therefore, the authoritative role of arbitrators in determining significant public personnel policies may be challenged as defying even the most generous notion of political accountability or representative government.

Some form of union security is allowed by law in many states. Mandatory dues, deductions, or fair-share deductions are provided for in about 50 percent of the states with comprehensive bargaining laws. These provisions are provided to circumvent what is known as the "free rider problem," in which a public employee can enjoy the benefits of employee representation without having to pay for its activities.

Finally, the ultimate weapon of public employees—the strike—is permitted in a few states. However, no state allows a general right to strike. Strikes are limited in a number of ways. Some states prohibit strikes by any public employee group whose absence could endanger public health, safety, or welfare; other states forbid strikes unless all available impasse-resolution procedures have been utilized and the union files a notice of intent to strike. Most states prohibit public employee strikes, with some of these legislating severe strike penalties such as fines, imprisonment, loss of employment, and decertification.

The advent of public-sector collective bargaining has significantly altered the political and administrative process of local governments. Local governments have lost unilateral authority over personnel management, decision-making power has been delegated to new private actors such as arbitrators and fact finders, and local civil service commissions have seen their responsibilities curtailed.

Many local governments have challenged state collective bargaining laws as illegal usurpations of fundamental local self-government rights to state administrative agencies. However, subordinate governmental units derive their power from the states. While many states have constitutional home rule provisions, state supreme courts have uniformly held that state-imposed public-sector collective bargaining laws represent the proper exercise of a state's police powers and therefore take precedence over home rule. Local personnel management has been viewed as a matter of statewide concern subject to the preemptive powers of state regulation.

Local civil service commissions have also been affected by the passage of collective bargaining laws. The activities of local civil service commissions have evolved to include the regulation of numerous personnel functions, such as wages, hours, working conditions, grievances, promotions, pensions, and vacations. State bargaining laws identify many of these issues as mandatory or permissive topics for negotiation.

In conclusion, public-sector collective bargaining has reduced the authority of public-sector managers and local governments while injecting new administrative and private entities into the personnel management process. Public employee relations boards, arbitrators, and fact finders have been entrusted with a great deal of authority over personnel issues. These types of transformations must be comprehended at a time when state and local public employment is increasing and personnel costs can account for as much as 80 percent of a local government's budget.

HEALTH CARE CONCERNS—AIDS

Acquired Immunodeficiency Syndrome (AIDS) will become one of the foremost workplace issues that municipal governments face as they approach the twenty-first century. According to the Centers for Disease Control and Prevention (CDC), 98 percent of people with AIDS are of working age and, furthermore, 80 percent of them are in the "prime" productive years of 20 to 44 (U.S. Department of Health and Human Services, July 1993). These statistics, in conjunction with the fact that fewer than 25 percent of people with AIDS are drug users, suggest that most people with AIDS could be working, if they are not already.

While estimates vary, it is reasonable to assume that 1 percent of the population in the United States has the human immunodeficiency virus (HIV), which causes AIDS (Slack, 1991). Most of these 2.6 million Americans remain unaware of their seropositive condition. Given that 1 percent of Americans has the HIV, we can estimate that 1 percent of the work force is also within the HIV spectrum. Because municipal government is the largest focal point of employment in the United States, with over 10.8 million people in its work force, we can reasonably assume that there are currently 108,000 municipal workers who have the AIDS virus. As with the general population, most of these municipal employees are unaware of their health status.

How much will the AIDS epidemic cost municipal governments? This will vary according to a variety of factors. Each seropositive individual will have different needs according to the stage of the disease he or she is experiencing: acute HIV, the asymptomatic stage, persistent generalized lymphadenopathy (PGL), or full-blown AIDS. Once a person's CD4 T-cell count has declined sufficiently (from a level of 1,200 to a level of 400) to permit AIDS-related illnesses, costs will also vary according to each individual disease.

For instance, the average annual cost of Bactrim Septra, a drug used to treat pneumocystic carinii pneumonia and toxoplasma gondii, is $400. The average annual cost for 3,200 daily milligrams of Acyclovir, used in the treatment of cytomegalovirus (CMV), is $5,115. The average annual cost of 600 milligram daily doses of Azidothymidine (AZT) and Didanosine (ddi), the only approved antiviral drugs, is $8,000 each. Typically, someone with AIDS will take both AZT and ddi.

Costs will also vary according to where treatment takes place and when it begins. Large urban locations, with a critical mass of people within the HIV spectrum, are able to minimize costs much more easily than are rural and isolated communities. If someone begins treatment at earlier stages of the disease, even at the asymptomatic stage, then pharmaceutical costs will be higher while hospitalization costs will be somewhat lessened. If someone delays treatment, hospitalization costs will be much higher and pharmaceutical costs will be lower at the beginning of symptoms. According to a Kaiser Permanente Northern California Region study (Hiatt et al., 1988), the average person with full-blown AIDS will experience 3.5 hospitalizations, with each visit lasting for approximately 40 days.

According to the AIDS Hotline of the CDC, the average annual health care cost is $10,000 for someone who is experiencing effects up through the PGL stage, and $38,300 for someone who has

AIDS. Yet these estimates do not accurately reflect the costs to local governments. These will depend on a number of factors, including the percentage of health care costs covered by group insurance, the amount of group life insurance, the types of reasonable accommodations made, and the salary and lifespan of the seropositive employee.

Table 2.5 offers an estimate of local government cost based on the following assumptions. First, the employee with HIV will live for twelve years. In this scenario, he or she is infected with HIV on January 1, 1994, and dies from AIDS on December 31, 2005. The person will spend the first seven years battling the virus up through the PGL stage. The final five years will be characterized as fighting full-blown AIDS. Second, as in the case of many people who are HIV-positive, the employee will be able to work well into the year of death. Third, the cost of reasonable accommodations will increase as the person progresses through the stages of the disease. Reasonable accommodations will range from providing flextime, to additional sick days, to job relocation, to working at home. Dollar amounts attributed to reasonable accommodations are based on estimates provided by the Job Accommodation Network (1992). Fourth, the person earns an annual salary of $25,000.

Table 2.5
Estimated Workplace Cost of AIDS

	Health Condition	Health Care Costs	Cost (and Number) of Sick Days		Reasonable Accommodation	Life Insurance	Total Costs
1994	HIV+	7,500	480.80	(5)	0	--	7,980.80
1995	HIV+	7,500	480.80	(5)	0	--	7,980.80
1996	HIV+	7,500	480.80	(5)	0	--	7,980.80
1997	PGL	7,500	480.80	(5)	100	--	8,080.80
1998	PGL	7,500	480.80	(5)	100	--	8,080.80
1999	PGL	7,500	673.12	(7)	500	--	8,673.12
2000	PGL	7,500	673.12	(7)	500	--	8,673.12
2001	AIDS	28,725	961.60	(10)	1,000	--	30,686.60
2002	AIDS	28,725	1,442.40	(15)	1,000	--	31,167.40
2003	AIDS	28,725	3,846.40	(40)	1,000	--	33,571.40
2004	AIDS	28,725	3,846.40	(40)	1,000	--	33,571.40
2005	DEATH	28,725	3,846.40	(40)	1,000	50,000	83,571.40
Total Municipal Government Cost per HIV Employee		196,725	17,693.44	(184)	6,200	50,000	270,018.44

Source: Compiled by the author.

This means that one sick day costs the city $96.16. Fifth, the city pays 75 percent of all health care costs through the group health plan. Hence, the city will pay for 75 percent of $10,000 in the HIV-positive stages through PGL, or $7,500, and 75 percent of the $38,300 in the AIDS stage, or $28,725. Sixth, the city agrees to pay $50,000 in the form of life insurance.

Several trends emerge from this hypothetical case. As reported in Table 2.5, it will cost municipal government approximately $270,000 for each employee who is in the HIV spectrum. While this cost may vary somewhat in different regions, the rate of increase will be relatively constant from year to year for the life of the employee. Further, expenses related to sick-day utilization will be a significant factor for each municipality. Sick day-related costs might easily match the cost of hiring one additional staff member, or at least a part-time worker, in many locations. Finally, reasonable accommodation expenses, the result of efforts mandated by the ADA, will be the least burdensome to municipal governments.

Assuming a 1 percent rate of infection among municipal employees, the numbers in Table 2.5 project a financial hardship for every city. The city of Mount Pleasant, Michigan, with a municipal work force of 100, can expect at least one employee to be HIV-positive. In order to stay within the boundaries of ADA, Mount Pleasant officials will have to find $270,018.44 in their city budgets over a period of twelve years. With 900 full-time employees, the city of Las Cruces, New Mexico, will need $2,430,166 for its estimated nine HIV-challenged employees. The city of Cleveland, with approximately 8,000 workers, will need to reserve $21,601,475 for its expected 80 seropositive employees. Los Angeles, with a work force of 25,000 employees, will need $67,504,610 to meet the needs of its estimated 250 workers who are in the HIV spectrum.

While such added expenses can often be passed on to the consumer in the private sector, typically this is not the case in government. Here the cost of AIDS will necessitate difficult decisions about the allocation of scarce resources from a limited and, in many cases, shrinking tax base. Many local governments will have to address the issue of maintaining current levels of services in the face of mounting costs for supporting the employment of seropositive individuals. The situation may soon arise in which citizens have to forgo financing preferred programs, such as in the areas of parks and recreation, public safety, or tourism and economic development, in order to reallocate scarce resources into personnel line-items. Programs that are either cut or reduced may not be viewed by the citizenry as luxury items, but rather as requisite services for maintaining or enhancing economic prosperity and the quality of life within the community. One consequence of the AIDS epidemic, therefore, is having to deal with community expectations about the level of services while meeting the health care requirements of members of the work force. This is a dilemma of growing urgency, given the fact that the epidemic continues to penetrate the fabric of all communities and regions.

CONCLUSIONS

The present and not-too-distant future provide many challenges for local government managers. They must deal with a variety of workplace issues in four areas: New Federalism, the legalities of the workplace, collective bargaining arrangements, and new crises like AIDS. To cope with these issues in an effective and compassionate manner, municipal managers must begin to acquire certain kinds of expertise and skills. The delineation and acquisition of the necessary managerial tools is the subject of the remaining chapters of this book.

Chapter 3

Training Theory and Approaches

Over the past decade, organizations in both the public and private sectors have become more aware of the need for increased attention to the training and retraining of their work forces. As discussed in Chapter 2, forces such as the New Federalism, legal issues associated with equal employment and affirmative action, evolving collective bargaining requirements, and various health issues have significantly altered the environment of local governments. In addition, vast changes in technology and information access, demographic changes in the work force, and fiscal pressures that consistently require governments to do more with less have altered the ways local governments do business. And although it is certainly true that training is often the first item cut from the budget in terms of fiscal austerity, it is also true that government agencies, like their counterparts in the private sector, are beginning to recognize the role that training can play in helping agencies meet the challenges brought on by these vast changes in their task environments (London and Wueste, 1992).

This chapter focuses on several broad issues associated with training. It begins by briefly examining the changing nature of training in work organizations, which has resulted in a need for an expanded definition of training. Next, the chapter discusses training from an organizational perspective and examines training as an organizational investment. In this section, a systems approach to training is presented as a perspective that can help cities enhance the effectiveness of their training programs. Finally, the chapter concludes with a brief look at managers and management training, specifying some training issues that will be salient for managers over the next decade.

A NEW ROLE FOR TRAINING IN ORGANIZATIONS

As organizations have expanded the role and mission of human resource development within organizations over the past twenty-five years, the nature of training has changed substantially. Traditionally, training was considered to be job-focused, limited to the teaching of skills and abilities needed by employees to perform specific tasks or to solve problems in particular settings. As such, it was differentiated from education, which was considered to be broader in scope, more oriented toward a range of future jobs and a career, and generally provided by institutions of higher learning (colleges and universities). Education "teaches general skills and knowledge *for the sake of a field or discipline*, rather than a particular job" (Van Wart, Cayer, and Cook, 1993:19, emphasis added). Traditionally, individuals obtained their education first and subsequently received training in the work environment based on their specific job needs.

Related to training and education is the concept of development. Formerly, development has focused more on the general growth of the individual than on a specific job or career need, and thus has emphasized the broader, long-term interests of the individual. As such, it has fallen under the domain of both work organizations and institutions of higher education.

More recently, the distinctions among training, education, and development have become somewhat blurred (Van Wart, Cayer, and Cook, 1993). As work organizations find themselves needing to help employees learn about new technologies and/or update knowledge and skills that have become obsolete as a result of changes in the disciplines and professions, training within organizations has, in many instances, begun to look more and more like what has traditionally been called education. For example, courses and workshops offered to update engineers on new methods of bridge construction, nurses on new drugs, or personnel specialists on changes in the law may closely resemble courses taken by these individuals some years before for academic credit. In addition, a substantial number of employees who do not have basic reading, writing, and arithmetic skills are being hired in areas where these skills are essential for their own safety.

On the academic side, there has been considerable debate over the content of academic courses offered by professional schools within institutions of higher education, such as schools of business, public administration or management, and so on. Academicians and practitioners argue over the extent to which educational programs offering degrees like the M.P.A. and M.B.A. should be concerned with job-specific relevance of course material, and whether education is beginning to look too much, or perhaps not enough, like training. Regardless of how this debate is resolved, it is clear that government agencies can no longer assume that employees' educational needs have been taken care of by the time an individual enters the work force or that training programs can be offered on a limited, as-needed basis. Similarly, employees must become more attuned to the notion of lifelong learning, rather than seeing each training course as a one-time experience that is job-related but disconnected from long-term goals. Instead, training within organizations must be seen as an integral part of a larger focus on the development of both the individual and the organization.

In Chapter 1, several definitions of training were presented, but we have thus far used the term without making explicit distinctions among training, education, and development as three areas of learning. It is necessary at this point to clarify how we are using the term. First, since our focus is on practitioners, we use the term "training" to refer to learning experiences designed to enhance the short-term and/or long-term job performance of individual employees. These experiences may be offered by the organization, exclusively for employees of the organization, or they may be offered by other institutions and may include employees of a wider variety of organizations. Second, as indicated above, we see training as an integral part of a development process. From the individual's perspective, a training course may be part of a long-term, continuous learning process. From the organization's perspective, the training course is part of an integral program of experiences offered to employees to enhance organizational performance. From both perspectives, training serves to further the individual's personal and professional growth. Finally, training may be provided in a broad spectrum of content areas that in some cases may overlap with knowledge and skill areas traditionally taught in academic institutions.

Given this expanded role for training within work organizations, it may be useful to identify the types of training typically provided by these organizations. Various taxonomies exist for classifying training experiences offered by work organizations. For example, some simply differentiate between technical and non-technical training. Others differentiate by target audience and/or occupational group. Van Wart, Cayer, and Cook (1993) differentiate among four general categories of training: technical (including procedural, mechanical, and professional); training that is not job-specific (basic and general skills); management (including supervisory, management, and executive); and employee enrichment. Table 3.1 presents a brief definition of each of these types. It is particularly interesting to note that two of the nine types of training—professional and basic skills—provide learning opportunities that were traditionally thought to be strictly in the domain of educational institutions. A third area, employee enrichment, provides learning opportunities that were also not considered to fall within the traditional purview of organizational training. We see the increasing availability of these types of training experiences in organizations as evidence of the changing nature of training within work organizations and the changing assumptions regarding the responsibilities agencies have for helping employees develop personally and professionally.

TRAINING AS AN ORGANIZATIONAL INVESTMENT

The second element of the definition of training provided above indicates that training should be seen as an integral part of a development process, from both the individual's and the organization's perspective. Indeed, for training to be truly effective, it must be tied to a broader organizational strategy for organizational improve-

Table 3.1
Types of Training Offered by Work Organizations

Technical	
Procedural:	Focuses on procedures, rules, laws, policies, or codes that are required for compliance with agency mandates and for coordination and work flow.
Mechanical:	Focuses on how things operate, how they are built, how they can be fixed when broken, and how they can be maintained.
Professional:	Focuses on the select knowledge, skills, and abilities needed by practicing professionals in performing their jobs. This type of training is generally more theory- and principle-driven than most other types of training.
Non-job-specific	
Basic:	Focuses on basic reading, writing, arithmetic, and communication skills. Includes both remedial and more advanced basic skills, such as public speaking.
General:	Focuses on making employees more effective outside their role as subject-area specialists, including interpersonal skills, problem solving, creativity, and basic management tools. Aims to improve employees' abilities to learn, to work with others, to adapt, and to be productive.
Management	
Supervisory:	Focuses on supervisors' direct interaction with subordinates and on getting work done by, with, or through other people.
Management:	Focuses on higher-level interpersonal/group process skills, such as labor relations and organizational climate. Also includes program management, budgeting and financial planning, risk management, decision-making and problem analysis, and information management.
Executive:	Focuses on the role of the organization in the public sector environment, including topics such as strategic planning, interagency teamwork, intergovernmental relations, management philosophy, and political and social trends. Is the most conceptual, broadest, and most externally oriented in the management training category.
Employee enrichment	Focuses on the needs, interests, and well-being of the learner; enhances personal capacity to focus on job skills or develops employee's long-range interests and well-being. Includes such areas as stress management, assertiveness training, career development, cultural diversity training, smoking cessation, memory improvement, and first aid.

Source: Adapted from Montgomery Van Wart, N. Joseph Cayer, and Steve Cook, Handbook of Training and Development for the Public Sector (San Francisco: Jossey-Bass Publishers, 1993), pp. 21-34.

ment. The necessity of linking training efforts with the organization's mission is becoming increasingly more evident (Eurich, 1985; Fisher, 1989; Latham, 1988; Miller, 1989). As Hussey argues:

There is a pressing need for a shift from the common idea that training should be for the improvement of the individual because this will benefit the [organization], to the concept that training should be for the benefit of the [organization] and this will benefit the individual. (1990:7)

Thus, as local government agencies examine their training needs, they first need to identify how training activities can be aligned with agency goals and then to base decisions regarding the budgeting and implementation of these activities on the extent to which such training programs are seen to contribute to the organization's mission (Cassner-Lotto and Associates, 1988).

In effect, organizations should view training activities as investments in both their and their employees' futures. Borrowing from the work of Chester Barnard, Frank Sherwood (1983) presents an analogy between material and human resources in organizations. He asserts that just as organizations spend money to maintain their capital assets because this has long-term pay-offs, they must also spend money to maintain their human assets in order to reap the same type of pay-offs. Maintaining human assets involves training and providing employees with opportunities for growth and development. He stresses that while maintenance involves short-term down-time, or time when the employees are not directly productive, this is a cost of doing business, an investment in the long-term health and viability of the organization.

Decisions about investments in training should be made with the same careful consideration as any other investment decision, and should be made in accordance with the organization's mission (Eurich, 1985). Linking training to the organization's mission necessitates that organizations take a systems view of training. Training activities should be examined from the perspective of their ability to influence individual job performance (and by extension, organizational effectiveness), rather than as isolated experiences that may or may not contribute to the organization's success. Organizations must therefore first identify what training and development experiences are needed to allow employees to contribute to the accomplishment of the organization's goals. Second, they must decide the optimal ways to deliver these experiences. They must also be able to assess whether these experiences have resulted in changes in actual work performance and use these assessments in future decisions about investments in training. Figure 3.1 presents this systems view of training, showing the three major components of training systems: needs assessment, design of training and development activities, and evaluation. Here we examine each of these components in greater depth.

Needs Assessments

In 1961, McGehee and Thayer wrote what is considered to be the first textbook on training in organizations, *Training in Business and Industry*. This book presented a three-fold approach to determining the types of training and development experiences that should be implemented, including organizational analyses, task analyses, and person analyses. More recently, others have

Figure 3.1
A Systems Approach to Training and Development

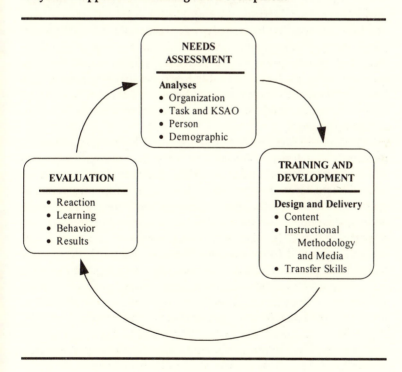

expanded on this framework to include demographic analyses (Latham, 1988) and to examine multiple levels of analysis associated with each of these components (Ostroff and Ford, 1989). Given the centrality of needs assessments to linking training and development activities to the agency's missions, it is important for managers to better understand the purpose of each of these components of needs assessments.

Organizational analyses focus on the components that influence the organization's ability to support training and development efforts. For example, what are the organization's goals? What resources are available for training and development efforts? What is the climate and what internal and external constraints are present in the environment (Goldstein, 1986)? Ostroff and Ford (1989) suggest that these analyses should also take into consideration the fact that different subunits, as well as different individuals, within the organization often have different goals and values. In addition, Wexley (1984) argues that analyses should be conducted to identify organizational units that are not performing at their optimal level. Such analyses would help identify whether training is the preferred solution to a performance gap, and whether it is reasonable to expect that employees who have participated in training and development activities will be able to use the newly acquired knowledge and skills when returning to work.

Task analyses focus on the knowledge, skills, abilities, and other personal characteristics (KSAOs) required to perform the agency's tasks. Again, Ostroff and Ford (1989) argue that such analyses should be performed at the organizational, subunit, and personal level of analysis. At the organizational level, the focus of these analyses would be "on the modal or most typical processes used to perform work" (p. 42). Because subunits within the organization often have different work processes and work flows, and individuals performing different jobs and tasks require different KSAOs, analyses at the subunit and individual levels of analysis should focus on the specific tasks at those levels. At the individual level, Campbell (1988) has noted that task analyses should explicitly define competent and expert performance. He suggests that multiple methods should be used to identify the important task elements of each job, as well as high and low performances.

It should be noted that to integrate training activities with the agency's strategic plan, these analyses should focus on KSAOs of potential future jobs as well as those of current jobs. This is especially crucial given the current debate over whether increasing levels of technology are increasing or decreasing the required levels of employee skills and education. Many researchers agree that the answers to this debate are not fully a function of the specific technology, but rather of how the organization chooses to use the technology (Bailey, 1990; Office of Technology Assessment, 1986). For example, word processing and other computing technology may de-skill secretarial and clerical jobs; "spell-checkers" reduce employees' need to spell; calculators reduce employees' needs to do basic math. However, these technologies may permit employees to do higher-level functions. For example, secretaries may take on more administrative functions or be asked to perform more complex tasks as they have greater time and increased abilities as a result of these technologies. Thus, task analyses need also to be integrated with organizational analyses to identify how technology will affect the nature of work and required KSAOs within the particular organizational culture. In addition, task analyses should be performed in conjunction with the agency's work force planning process to determine, for example, the level of KSAOs of individuals to be recruited from outside the organization (Ban, Faerman, and Riccucci, 1992).

Person analyses focus on the needs of the individual, identifying the KSAOs possessed by the particular individual. Ostroff and Ford (1989) argue that such analyses should be extended to the subunit and organizational level, allowing the organization to see from a broader perspective the KSAOs that exist across the organization. Most person analyses assume a discrepancy model, comparing actual behavior with ideal or expected behaviors, and thus need to be integrated with a task analysis that has identified the ideal or expected behaviors. One important issue associated with such analyses is: Who determines what KSAOs an individual possesses? Self-assessments, while convenient, often have low validity (Wexley, 1984). Moreover, individuals may be prone to identify their desired, rather than needed, training areas. Since adults tend to resist "being sent" to training (Knowles, 1987), it is generally preferable for employees to be involved in the assessment of their training needs. Research has shown that self-assessments have greatest validity when employees expect that the results will be compared with other criterion measures; when employees are guaranteed anonymity; when employees have previous experience with self-evaluation, as in performance evaluation; and when they are asked to make relative, rather than absolute, judgments (Wexley, 1984). As in other areas of data collection, it is preferable, where possible, to use multiple sources, including the individual, his or her supervisor, as well as peers and staff, as appropriate.

As discussed above, demographic analyses have recently emerged as a fourth component of needs assessment (Latham, 1988). Demographic analyses focus on the specific training needs of populations of workers. For example, demographic analyses have been used to examine technical managers' (i.e., engineers and other scientists) general supervisory and management training needs (Katz and Rosen, 1987), women managers' communication skills training needs (Berryman-Fink, 1984) and older workers' technological and management training needs (Tucker, 1985). As local government agencies find themselves dealing with more diverse populations as a result of nationwide changes in demographic trends, they may also need to perform demographic analyses to determine the sensitivity of various groups in dealing with citizens of different demographic groups.

Design of Training Activities

Two related issues must be addressed in the design of training activities. The first is the question of how a given course should be delivered. Who should be asked (or allowed) to participate? Where should the course be held—on site or at another facility? What types of learning tools or approaches should be incorporated into the program? These are issues associated with the classroom experience. A second, but perhaps more important, issue is the creation of a learning experience that optimizes the transfer of knowledge and skills from the classroom to the work environment. It is not enough for trainees to learn new knowledge and skills; they must be able and willing (and ultimately supported by others in their work environment) to use new abilities on their job. Newstrom (1986) argues that too much money and attention are spent on the design and delivery of training and not enough on efforts to increase the transfer of training to the work environment. Invoking the Pareto principle, he suggests that "even a modest allocation of time, creativity and effort might induce tremendous payoffs . . . [and] become responsible for 80 percent of [the] results" (pp. 35–36). This suggests that care needs to be taken in designing the delivery of training activities so that they allow individuals to feel that they know how and when to use the specific knowledge and skills acquired and also that they are able to use the knowledge and skills in the appropriate situation.

Design of training activities in work organizations requires attention to the principles of andragogy, or the "art and science of helping adults learn" (Knowles, 1987). Knowles argues that, in many ways, adults learn differently from children, and that training and development for adults need to account for these differences. He identifies several assumptions upon which andragogical models of learning are based. First, adults have a need to know why they should learn something. Thus, employees need to see training experiences as relevant to their current work environments or at least potentially relevant to a future work environment. Second, adults have a deep need to be self-directing. As in general work situations, employees prefer to feel that they have some control over their lives and have some responsibility for making decisions that affect their futures. Training and development experiences often put the employee in the position of being dependent on someone else (the trainer) and may thus create feelings of inner conflict that result in decreased motivation or withdrawal from the situation. To avoid this reaction, employees need to be active participants in the learning process.

Third, managers and trainers must recognize that adult employees have a greater volume and different quality of experience than youths. Training experiences should build on and affirm the experiences that employees bring to the situation. Crapo (1986) argues that the best trainers do not train, in the classical sense, but rather facilitate, providing opportunities for the members of the group to learn from each other. Fourth, adults become ready to learn when they experience in their life situation a need to be able to perform more effectively and satisfyingly. This assumption builds on the first and second assumptions, and suggests that adult learners need not only to be active participants in the learning process, but also participants in decisions regarding their involvement in training and development experiences. Employees who are "sent" to training will rarely be motivated to learn, unless they themselves see the need for growth and improvement in that particular area. Finally, adults enter into a learning experience with a task-centered (or problem-centered or life-centered) orientation to learning. Building on the first assumption, adults need to see learning experiences as relevant to their jobs, and the specific problems or issues that they must deal with on their job.

In the design of training and development activities, a wide variety of instructional media is available to trainers and managers, such as on-the-job-training, programmed instruction, satellite teleconferencing, computer-assisted instruction, and so on (Campbell, 1988; Goldstein, 1986; Latham, 1989). With recent changes in information, telecommunication, and other computer-based technologies, there has been an increased ability to offer courses using resources from distant sites (Bernold and Finkelstein, 1987). As we move into the twenty-first century, these technologies will create the potential to greatly enhance the range of training experiences available to local governments, particularly in areas that are geographically isolated and have relatively small training staffs.

In the classroom, there is a wide variety of instructional techniques that can be used, including lectures, case studies, simulations, role-play exercises, fish-bowl exercises, and small and large group discussions. Regardless of the technique or media used, trainers and managers should be aware of several important principles that will optimize the transfer of training. First, trainees should be active participants in the learning process. Second, they should have the opportunity to practice knowledge and skills in a scenario that closely resembles the actual job situation. Third, participants should receive feedback on their behaviors. Fourth, participants should have the opportunity to set goals that are realistic. Fifth, mechanisms for supporting the application of new knowledge and skills should be created in the employees' work environments. Superiors and peers should be involved and trained to look for and reinforce the use of newly acquired knowledge and skills.

Finally, employees should be given skills that enhance their abilities to transfer learning to the work environment (Campbell,

1988). As indicated above, the ultimate issue in training design is whether training participants are able to transfer newly acquired knowledge and skills to the work situation. Research in the area of social learning theory and self-efficacy (Bandura, 1977a, 1977b) has shown that individuals who are high in self-efficacy—the belief that one has the ability to take control of situations and influence events in a positive way—are better able to transfer learning from the training to the work environment. Moreover, it has been shown that self-efficacy can be increased by such techniques as active participation, feedback, and goal-setting (Latham, 1988). This conclusion suggests that trainers should consider assessing such individual variables as self-efficacy in their needs assessments, and that the design of training experiences should account for such individual differences, using techniques to increase self-efficacy, as appropriate (Campbell, 1988).

Evaluation

Increasingly, government agencies are being asked to become more accountable, to justify the existence of programs in terms of costs and performance factors. This concern has led to an increased focus on evaluation of training and development activities in organizations.

A basic model for understanding evaluation has been proposed by Kirkpatrick (1987). This model identifies four criteria for evaluating the effectiveness of training programs: reaction, learning, behavior, and results (or impact). Reaction is the most typical evaluation, delivered at the completion of most training and educational programs. It may be defined as the extent to which the participants liked the experience. Although reaction evaluations are sometimes discredited by human resource development specialists and pejoratively referred to as "happiness indexes" or "smile sheets," they can be used effectively to examine different aspects of participants' reactions to the course (Faerman and Ban, 1993; Robinson and Robinson, 1989). For example, reaction surveys may ask whether participants found the material to be relevant, the instructor performed well, the location was convenient and conducive to learning, the training was appropriate for their level of knowledge, and so on. In addition, while reaction evaluations are generally conducted immediately after the completion of the course, they can also be conducted as part of a follow-up evaluation, from six months to a year following course completion, asking participants to comment on such issues as course relevance and usefulness of course material to job performance. The key to making reaction evaluations useful is to be certain of the type of information wanted and the purpose of gathering this information (Robinson and Robinson, 1989).

Learning refers to participants' cognitive, rather than affective, reaction to the course. Did they understand and absorb the principles and concepts presented? Are they more knowledgeable about the specific content area at the completion of the course than they were at the beginning? Although this is rarely examined in most types of training programs, it is particularly useful when training courses are designed to provide specific knowledge that must later be applied to a work situation. Learning evaluations are generally conducted through written examinations. Computer-assisted instruction may include learning evaluations as an integral part of the training experience.

Behavior generally involves the transfer of classroom learning to changes in behavior on the job, although some have used the term to refer to participants being able to perform the appropriate behaviors in the classroom situation as well. In addition, some use the term to refer to non-observable results, such as changes in attitudes or cognitive approaches, such as the use of a particular problem-solving technique or the making of decisions based on a particular management philosophy (Robinson and Robinson, 1989). Evaluations of changes in behavior are much more difficult to conduct than those of reaction or learning because, to be effective, they should involve a systematic appraisal of job performance, both before and after completion of the course. Where possible, appraisal should be performed by several individuals, including those receiving the training, their superior(s), their subordinates, and/or peers. Where feasible, it should also include a control group that has not received the training, for comparison.

Finally, impact or results evaluations are defined in terms of the organizational, rather than individual, changes that occur as a result of the training program. Such changes may include increased productivity, reduced costs, improved morale, enhanced delivery of services, and so on. One technique of results evaluation that has recently received greater attention is utility analysis (Carr, 1988; Cascio, 1989; Schmidt, Hunter, and Pearlman, 1982). This technique, originally developed to estimate the impact of selection procedures on job performance, has also proved useful for estimating the dollar impact of training programs. Carr argues that utility analyses can help human resource managers to document more effectively the impact of training and thus demonstrate the centrality of training to organizational effectiveness. Such evaluations are, however, even more difficult to conduct than are evaluations of behavioral change. Moreover, because of the multiple factors that influence organizational effectiveness, some have argued that it is not reasonable to try to identify and measure organizational-level changes produced by training (Campbell, 1988).

An increased emphasis on accountability would suggest that trainers and managers need to focus more on behavior and results, rather than reaction and learning, as evaluation criteria. Unfortunately, organizations and their employees often see evaluation as peripheral to training and development efforts, and argue that money allocated to extensive evaluation efforts results in reduced resources available for actual training. Agencies need to recognize, however, that evaluation should not be an end product; training and development programs should not be evaluated as either good or bad (Wexley, 1984). Rather, as Figure 3.1 shows, evaluation should be used as feedback, to provide information that would allow for improvement in the program so that these programs can become more effective with respect to their contribution to the agency's mission. As such, evaluation is an investment in the training process, a component as essential as curriculum design in developing a quality program.

MANAGERS AND MANAGEMENT TRAINING ISSUES

The changing nature of work and the changing nature of the work force present a number of challenges for tomorrow's public managers. Consequently, a major challenge for local government agencies will be to provide the appropriate training and development experiences for its managers. The vast majority of managerial positions in the federal, state, and local governments are filled by individuals who have been chosen for their positions on the basis of technical qualifications in a specialized profession or career field (Flanders, 1989; U.S. General Accounting Office, 1989). The one relevant exception to this norm is, of course, city managers, whose profession is management. In most other cases, management is considered to be a second, and often a secondary, profession, for most public managers. While this has advantages with respect to managers' substantive knowledge of various policy areas, it also has important drawbacks. As Flanders notes, "For the most part, the orientations, values, and training and education provided in many professions do not offer a good foundation for carrying out or even understanding public management responsibilities" (1989:430).

Because most public managers tend to see management as their "second profession," it is especially important for local government agencies to provide systematic training and development experiences for managers. Using a common competency base for managers at all levels will help managers understand how management skills change as they move up the organizational hierarchy. This assessment should include the similarities and differences among the KSAOs required at different levels of management (Faerman and Peters, 1991; Flanders, 1989).

In addition, as suggested above, managers need to have new skills to perform effectively in a work environment with changing technologies and changing demographics. Bozeman and Rahm (1989) have argued that public managers increasingly need to keep aware of societal technological change. Managing a changing work environment, however, implies a need not only for increased knowledge of the technology, but also for increased self-awareness and interpersonal skills. First, managers will need to be aware of their own stereotypes and biases. Sterns and Doverspike (1989) have found that older workers are often given differential access to training and retraining programs because of managers' assumptions regarding these workers' abilities or motivation levels. An awareness of these stereotypes and biases may help managers to refrain from and prevent discrimination against women, people of color, people with disabilities, and older workers and to maximize participation of all members of the work force. Second, managers will need to be better able to adapt to change and to help employees adapt to change. Third, they will also need to be able to deal with interpersonal and intergroup conflict that may result from a more culturally diverse work force. Fourth, they will need to be better mentors and coaches, providing on-the-job training and motivating employees to develop their own potential. Chapters 4 and 5 will discuss some of these issues in greater depth.

CONCLUSIONS

This chapter has focused on general issues associated with training, focusing on the changing role of training in work organizations and the need for local government agencies to take a systems perspective in developing training programs. It is clear that as we move into the twenty-first century, training and retraining will play a central role in helping organizations adapt to the changes they are experiencing in their social, political, economic, and technological environments (London and Wueste, 1992). In order for training to provide the greatest benefit to local governments, however, agencies will need to understand the strategic value of training and coordinate training strategy with agency and, more generally, local government strategies. Local governments will need to understand that training and development activities are more than employee benefits; they are investments in the agencies' and cities' own futures. City governments will need to integrate the planning of training and development programs with their centralized strategic planning activities, focusing on how the nature of work is likely to change over the next ten to twenty years, as well as on how the environment of local government will change over this period.

In addition, cities will need to develop policies regarding the role of training in their career management systems. For example, the Report of the Task Force on Education and Training to the National Commission on the Public Service (1989)—also known as the Volcker Commission—suggested that the U.S. Office of Personnel Management (OPM) help agencies design clear paths for advancement to the Senior Executive Service. It also suggested that OPM adopt a policy requiring regular training for all professional employees. Career planning and continuous learning should not, however, be a concern just for professionals and upper-level managers; they are necessary for all levels of the organizational hierarchy. Almost thirty years ago, Jay Forrester argued that "some 25 percent of the total working time of all persons in the corporation should be devoted to preparation for their future roles. . . . The educational program must become an integral part of corporate life, not a few weeks or months once a lifetime at another institution" (1965:16). Rapid technological changes can bring rapid technological obsolescence. It has been estimated that nearly half the jobs in the U.S. economy are currently transformed or replaced every five to eight years (Miller, 1989) and that in the near future, employers will have to retrain office workers five to eight times during their career (Wexley, 1984). Clearly, both local governments and their employees will have to become more comfortable with the notion of continuous learning for all employees.

Government agencies must also be willing to retrain workers for new jobs when their old jobs become obsolete. While career planning and continuous learning can provide some degree of safety against obsolescence, one cannot ignore the fact that rapid technological changes will result in radical transformation or total replacement of some current jobs. In essence, the job changes caused by technological advances will, in many cases, require more than new knowledge and skills; they will require new socialization, new attitudes, new values, and new assumptions (Miller, 1989). In addition, given the decreasing number of entry-level workers, retraining workers is likely to prove more cost-effective than recruiting and hiring new people.

Finally, local governments will need to learn to be more creative about finding and using financial resources to fund training activities. In some cases, city governments may be able to coordinate with other local governments that are geographically close. In other cases, they may be able to get support from local colleges and universities. Local governments may also be able to form partnerships with local businesses to provide opportunities that will benefit the two groups. Finally, in some cases, local governments may come to rely on computing and telecommunication technologies that can bring distant resources close.

Chapter 4

Current and Future Training and Assistance Needs

Because municipalities operate within an environment of fluctuation and turbulence, city officials enjoy only a minimal level of control over conditions and events that have a direct bearing on the future of their organizations and communities. Changes in social demographic patterns, community preferences, federal and state laws, and unrelenting expectations for greater efficiency in both budget and finance all tend to limit the ability of city managers and mayors to make accurate forecasts about unforeseen issues and crises. Nevertheless, it is important to examine the views of local government officials about what they think will be needed in the future, as well as about what they think is currently needed.

This chapter looks at current and future training and assistance needs of municipal governments. In the first section, the perceptions of city managers and mayors about current training needs are reviewed. In addition, this section looks at the effects of several social and structural variables on perceived training and assistance needs. The second section of this chapter explores perceptions of city managers and mayors regarding training and assistance needs as their cities prepare to enter the twenty-first century.

PERCEPTIONS OF CITY MANAGERS AND MAYORS REGARDING CURRENT NEEDS

In 1989 a questionnaire was administered to a random sample of 500 city managers and mayors, drawn from the list of cities included in the 1988 volume of *The Municipal Year Book*. With up to three mailings used, 340 local government practitioners (68 percent of the total) returned usable questionnaires.

Respondents were evenly split between city managers (48.5 percent) and mayors (51.5 percent). Cities included in this sample were fairly representative of the larger population. The staff size of city government ranged from 0 (one case) to 5,500 (one case) full-time professional and administrative personnel, with a mean of 90 and a median of 10. City populations ranged from 2,000 (one case) to over 1,000,000 (two cases), with the mean and median community size being 35,000 and 10,000, respectively. Table 4.1 provides the frequency distributions for the municipalities based on population.

City managers and mayors were asked to rate their current city government's information, training, and assistance needs in thirty functional areas using a five-point Likert-type scale (1 = Least Needed; 5 = Most Needed). The survey instrument can be found in Appendix A. Responses to the survey indicated that training and assistance needs of local government practitioners are quite diverse. Table 4.2 reports mean ratings across the entire sample. Of

Table 4.1
Municipalities in Sample by Population

	Number of Municipalities
less than 10,000	159
10,000 to 50,000	147
50,000 to 100,000	11
100,000 to 200,000	12
200,000 to 1 million	9
1 million or more	2
Total	**340**

Source: Compiled by the author.

the thirty areas, those that received a mean score of 3.0 or better include human resource management (personnel performance, disciplinary practices, and merit principles and practices), dealing with the organization's external environment (community relations and working with elected officials), and maintenance and operations activities (computer literacy and program evaluation).

To examine the effects that local government's social and structural environment may have on the level and types of training and assistance needed, we looked at three background variables: community size, form of government, and access to universities.

First, we asked, "Do the training needs of local governments differ according to community size?" While not all findings are consistent (Cigler, 1990), previous studies suggest the existence of differences between larger, more urban local governments and those found in smaller, more rural communities. David R. Morgan, for instance, suggests that the large city environment creates a "special context in which urban management functions" (1989:4). A greater concern for acquiring and utilizing management tools is shown by officials of larger municipalities (Poister and Streib, 1989a). Furthermore, government staffs of smaller communities tend to be less professionally trained than those in larger cities (Brown, 1980). Several studies (Dillman and Tremblay, 1977; Cigler, 1984) indicate that rural and small town governments have felt the effects of federal government cutbacks much more harshly than larger cities, primarily because small towns have less flexibility in budgetary and fiscal matters (MacManus and Pammer, 1990). Because local governments of smaller communities are hampered by fiscal and professional limitations, we should expect them to be in greater need of information, training, and assistance than are larger municipalities, which tend to have greater access to a variety of capacity-building tools.

Table 4.3 shows the training and assistance areas with the highest (3-point range) mean scores broken down by community size. The table shows that with the exception of "working with elected officials" and "program evaluation," city managers and mayors from smaller communities (30,000 and under in population) indicate a slightly greater perceived need for training and assistance than do city managers and mayors of larger communities. Differences should be kept in perspective, as is indicated by the results of

Table 4.2
**Perceived Information, Training, and Assistance Needs of Local
Government Practitioners**

	Mean Rating
Personnel Performance	3.27
Disciplinary Practices	3.13
Community Relations	3.11
Working with Elected Officials	3.10
Computer Literacy	3.08
Program Evaluation	3.00
Merit Principles and Practices	3.00
Organizational Development and Work Relations	2.96
Public Works and Capital Financing	2.94
Writing and Oral Communication Skills	2.90
Safety and Health Conditions	2.88
Labor Relations	2.86
Maintenance Functions	2.84
Grant Writing	2.82
Position Classification	2.81
Budgeting	2.77
Local Government Documents and Reports	2.74
"How-To" Manuals	2.73
Personnel Staffing	2.73
Contract Management	2.65
Census Data	2.64
Statistical and Data Analysis	2.56
Cash Management	2.50
Local Government Data Bank	2.46
Accounting	2.46
EEO and Affirmative Action	2.34
Federal and State Government Depository	2.05
Professional Books and Journals	2.04
Legislative Histories	2.03

Source: Compiled by the author.

Table 4.3
Mean Rating of Highest-Ranked Local Government Needs by Size of Community

	Size of Community	
	30,000 or less	More than 30,000
Personnel Performance	3.28	3.25
Disciplinary Practices	3.18	2.89
Community Relations	3.13	3.03
Working with Elected Officials	3.08	3.16
Computer Literacy*	3.19	2.63
Program Evaluation	2.99	3.06
Merit Principles and Practices	3.03	2.87

Source: Compiled by the author.
*Statistically significant difference between two groups at $p < .001$.

the t-test of differences between means for the two categories of population. These differences are only marginal, with the only statistically significant differences seen in needs for computer literacy.

Second, we asked: "Does the structure of local government have a bearing on its perceived training needs?" Here we looked at two different structures, the council-manager and mayor-council forms of government. The literature suggests that city managers tend to behave differently from mayors of non-council-manager cities (Goldstein and Ehrenberg, 1976). City managers tend to manage organizations in a more "businesslike" fashion (Morgan, 1989), placing greater emphasis on limiting taxation and expenditure levels (Lineberry and Fowler, 1967) and finding innovative fiscal alternatives, such as the use of municipal enterprises (Rubin, 1988). While all studies do not concur (Morgan and Pelissero, 1980), overall findings suggest that city managers place a higher priority on such concepts as effectiveness, efficiency, and equity in organizational performance than do mayors in municipalities with other forms of government (Abney and Lauth, 1986). More so than mayors, city managers tend to be willing to experiment with new managerial tools (Poister and Streib, 1989a). Based on the findings of previous research, therefore, we should expect the chief administrative officers of council-manager governments to be more concerned with acquiring new, innovative tools. However, they might have less need for training in more traditional "tried and true" tools that increase productivity and performance.

Table 4.4 shows that, slightly more so than mayors, city managers perceive a greater need for training and education needs. The exceptions here are in the areas of "computer literacy" and "merit principles and practices." As with Table 4.3, the t-test results verify that most differences between the views of chief executive officers of council-manager and mayor-council forms of government are not statistically significant. Statistically significant differences do exist, however, in perceived needs for training in the areas of personnel performance, community relations, and working with elected officials.

The third question we asked was: Does access to university-based public-sector outreach units have a bearing on the training needs of local governments? The tradition of American higher education is the creation of new knowledge that will contribute to educating students and improving the human condition. The notion of applying new knowledge to meet the direct needs of the

Table 4.4
Mean Rating of Highest-Ranked Local Government Needs by Form of Government

| | Form of Government | |
	Mayor	City Manager
Personnel Performance*	3.13	3.42
Disciplinary Practices	3.09	3.17
Community Relations*	2.98	3.25
Working with Elected Officials*	2.95	3.25
Computer Literacy	3.14	3.02
Program Evaluation	2.91	3.10
Merit Principles and Practices	3.07	2.93

Source: Compiled by the author.
*Statistically significant difference between two groups at $p < .05$.

citizenry is most apparent in agricultural colleges at land-grant universities. Yet most universities, public and private, espouse a broader, public service mission, and some have established institutes and centers for this purpose. In addition, in the past decade there has been a blurring of the distinction between training and education, as work organizations have attempted to keep employees up to date on technological changes, as well as changes in principles of professional practice, and institutions of higher education have attempted to make education relevant by including practical examples and applications of principles on credit-bearing courses (Van Wart, Cayer, and Cook, 1993).

Studies to date provide disappointing findings about the use of universities to meet the training needs of local governments. Practitioners tend to rely more on other external sources, especially private-sector consulting firms, than on university-based outreach units (Whorton, Gibson, and Dunn, 1986). Local government's failure to utilize academic resources may be due in part to university presidents' low priority for outreach activities (Dunn, Gibson, and Whorton, 1985), as well as discrepancies between the goals of outreach unit directors and the needs of the public sector practitioners (Whorton, Gibson, and Dunn, 1986). These studies, however, have not focused on the relationship between local government's access to university-based outreach units and the actual levels or needs for information, training, and assistance. It is quite possible, therefore, that local governments with access to universities have fewer information, training, and assistance needs than do local governments without such access.

Respondents were asked: "To your knowledge, has your city ever been contacted by a college/university to address your training/assistance/information needs?" As seen in Table 4.5, respondents who have been contacted by university-based outreach units perceive a slightly greater need for training and assistance than those who have no contact with such academic units. Those not in contact with universities perceive slightly greater training needs in the areas of "computer literacy" and "merit principles and practices." As in the above analyses, these findings suggest only marginal differences, and no differences are statistically significant.

Responses to the thirty information, training, and assistance items were then regrouped into five dimensions or scales of local

Table 4.5
Mean Rating of Highest-Ranked Local Government Needs by Access to Universities

	Contacted by University-Based Outreach Unit	
	Yes	*No*
Personnel Performance	3.31	3.17
Disciplinary Practices	3.10	3.08
Community Relations	3.21	2.99
Working with Elected Officials	3.16	3.00
Computer Literacy	2.97	3.21
Program Evaluation	3.10	2.85
Merit Principles and Practices	2.98	2.99

Source: Compiled by the author.

government needs: (1) information and library usage; (2) maintenance and operations activities; (3) fiscal-related issues; (4) human resource management concerns; and (5) issues concerning the external environment. Statistical analyses showed these scales to have a moderate level of internal consistency.[1] Further analyses were then performed to examine the statistical relationships between the five dimensions and the three environmental factors discussed above—community background, form of government, and access to university-based outreach units. For access to university-based outreach units, distance to the university was examined, as was whether or not the city had been contacted by the university. The results are reported in Table 4.6.

Table 4.6 shows that the most influential factor seems to be community population. Smaller communities tend to need greater assistance in the areas of information, organizational maintenance and operation, fiscal matters, and human resources management concerns. Form of government appears to have only a marginal impact on needs. Mayors are more likely than city managers to perceive assistance needs in the information area, while city managers are more likely to need assistance in dealing with the external environment. With respect to contact with university-based

Table 4.6
Analysis of Statistical Relationships Between Background Factors and Needs Dimensions

	Community Size		Form of	Access to Universities	
	Population[b]	Employees[a]	Government[b]	Contact[b]	Distance[a]
Information/Library Usage	4.46***	−.14*	2.19*	3.41***	.07
Maintenance and Operation	3.81***	−.09	.82	2.23*	.08
Fiscal Issues	4.06***	−.11	1.70	2.70**	.16**
Human Resources	2.72**	−.08	−1.04	.31	.07
External Environment	.11	.11	−2.45*	−1.52	.12*

Source: Compiled by the author.
[a] Pearson correlation coefficient.
[b] Student's t-test statistic.
*p < .05; ** p < .01; *** p < .001.

outreach programs, it appears that a slight pattern exists, with the perceived need for training or assistance in the information, fiscal, and organizational maintenance and operation dimensions being greater for those respondents who have never been contacted by university-based outreach units. Somewhat differently, those officials whose city halls are a greater distance from college campuses perceive slightly more need for training and assistance in the external environment and fiscal areas.

In summary, findings of this survey indicate that local government practitioners are concerned with a variety of training and assistance issues. With the highest mean score at 3.27 (using a 5-point scale, where 5 = "most needed"), however, no sense of urgency or crisis about the quality or quantity of the managerial training and assistance available to local government is indicated by these findings. The fact that mean ratings did not approach the five-point maximum lends credence to Poister and Streib's (1989a:242) contention that a "ceiling effect" may be taking place. Some managerial tools are becoming quite commonplace, leading local government practitioners to reach a "saturation point at which interest in them simply levels off."

While the impact of form of government and access to universities is mixed and marginal, there are some differences between large and small communities. The distinction, however, appears to be one of degree and not of direction. That is, the training and assistance needs of both settings are similar in terms of specific tools; the needs of local government in smaller settings are some-what greater, perhaps reflecting slightly smaller resources.

In the case of newer tools available to the practitioner, such as with the library and information resources, low mean ratings may reflect a lack of awareness of the applicability of particular information and library-based tools to local government problem-solving. The fact that more than half (51 percent) of the respondents in the study have never been contacted by a university-based outreach unit suggests that local government officials may be somewhat uninformed about the kinds of services that are available at good university (public administration) libraries. The fact that those who have been contacted by universities also have less of a need for such services may lend support to this line of thinking.

PERCEPTIONS OF CITY MANAGERS AND MAYORS REGARDING FUTURE NEEDS

As indicated earlier, municipalities operate in an environment of fluctuation and turbulence, where city officials enjoy only minimal control over conditions and events that have a direct bearing on the future of their organizations and communities. It is thus important to examine changing training and assistance needs, and to examine what mayors and city managers expect their needs to be as we move to the year 2000. We thus asked respondents to examine the list of thirty functional areas and to identify the five areas in which they think their organization "will have the greatest training, assistance, or information need during the next ten years."

The majority (55.6%) of city managers and mayors listed one of six training areas in which they believe their respective municipalities' greatest need will fall within the next ten years. These top selections are reported in Table 4.7.

Four patterns emerge from their responses. First, municipal officials seem equally concerned with acquiring additional skills that will help them meet two types of responsibilities—dealing with the external environment and working with internal operations. With respect to the external environment, local government officials indicated that they need to acquire skills in the areas of community relations, program evaluation, and public works. With

Table 4.7
Areas in Which Local Government Officials Anticipate the Greatest Need for Training, Assistance, and Information by the Year 1999

	Percentage of Local Government Officials Selecting Area
Computer Literacy	13.2
Budgeting	12.8
Community Relations	7.8
Program Evaluation/Needs Assessment	7.8
Public Works/Capital Financing	7.0
Writing and Oral Communication Skills	7.0
Total	**55.6**

Source: Compiled by the author.

respect to internal operations, officials identified the areas of computer literacy, budgeting, and communication skills as ones that will help them manage the workplace more effectively.

Second, while city managers and mayors may be equally concerned with improving their capacity to deal with the external world and internal workings of the organization, future training and education needs of municipal governments may be more disparate and unique than current expectations (Poister and Streib, 1989a). For instance, a significant proportion (44.4%) of practitioners in this survey did not choose among the six areas listed in Table 4.7 as their respective municipalities' "most needed area" for training in the future. Quite to the contrary, respondents' preferences seem to be evenly dispersed among the remaining twenty-four areas outlined in the survey instrument. As reported in Table 4.7, moreover, no training area came close to being designated as "most needed" by even one in five practitioners.

The third pattern to emerge from the findings in Table 4.7 suggests that the type of training and education "most needed" in the future may not always emanate from the traditional "human relations" model. With the one exception of having better relations with the community, building technical capacity within the organization seems to be a higher priority than enhancing interpersonal skills. What practitioners seem to be saying is that they believe they will need more of the "nuts and bolts" type of training and education in the future, and less of the "warm and fuzzy" kind that tends to dominate training curricula today. This view may help to explain the rather high rate of failure and dissatisfaction reported among practitioners with contemporary human relations programs and retreats (Gabris, 1989).

Fourth, half of the areas listed as future needs are also areas in which city managers and mayors believe they are currently in need of assistance (see discussion above). Current and future needs tend to blend in the areas of computer literacy, community relations, and program evaluation. Such an overlap between current and future assistance needs suggests that local government officials consider the acquisition of expertise in certain functional areas an ongoing process. Those skills need to be reintroduced routinely for the benefit of new personnel and updated periodically so that all employees have an opportunity to take advantage of recent technological advances.

Again, it is important to ask whether factors such as form of government or size of community have a bearing on perceptions about future training and education needs of practitioners. As discussed earlier, previous research on this subject suggests that city managers are more concerned with the operation of government (Morgan, 1989), while mayors tend to be more concerned about the delivery of service to various groups within the community (Abney and Lauth, 1986). More than mayors, city managers also tend to express a slightly greater recognition of and respect for the need for further training and education (Slack, 1990). They are also more willing than mayors to experiment with new managerial tools (Poister and Streib, 1989a).

Findings of other studies also indicate key differences in capacity between governments of larger and smaller communities. Local governments in smaller settings tend to be in greater need of additional professional training (Brown, 1980). While the type of assistance need may be similar to that of urban governments, the degree to which education and training activities are needed seems to be somewhat greater in smaller towns (Slack, 1990). Moreover, throughout this past decade, city halls in smaller communities have felt the impact of federal cutbacks more intensely than their counterparts in metropolitan areas, primarily because of large city government's greater flexibility in finding alternative funding sources and strategies (MacManus and Pammer, 1990).

As reported in Table 4.8, survey findings indicate that type of government, as well as size of community, can affect municipal officials' perceptions about future training, information, and assistance needs. The table shows that budgeting was most often selected as the area of greatest need by mayors who responded to the survey (16.1%), whereas computer literacy was the area most often identified by the city managers (15.8%). With respect to the other four areas identified in Table 4.7, a greater percentage of city managers perceive community relations, program evaluation, and writing and oral communication skills as their greatest need, whereas mayors perceive greater needs in public works and capital financing.

Community size also has some bearing on officials' perceptions of future needs. More than respondents from smaller communities, chief administrative officers from municipalities with populations over 30,000 are concerned about enhancing skills that will make them more effective in dealing with forces "external" to the organization: community relations, program evaluations/needs assessment, and writing/oral communication skills. On the other hand, mayors and city managers from smaller towns express a slightly greater need for acquiring skills that will make their organizations internally more efficient: computer literacy, budgeting, and public works.

Table 4.8
Areas in Which Local Government Officials Anticipate the Greatest Need for Training, Assistance, and Information by Form of Government and Size of Community*

	Form of Government		Size of Community	
	Mayor	City Manager	30,000 or less	More than 30,000
Computer Literacy	10.9	15.8	14.6	7.8
Budgeting	16.1	9.2	15.0	3.9
Community Relations	5.1	10.8	6.8	11.8
Program Evaluation/Needs Assessment	5.8	10.0	6.3	13.7
Public Works/Capital Financing	8.8	5.0	8.3	2.0
Writing and Oral Communication Skills	5.1	9.2	6.8	7.8

Source: Compiled by the author.
* Percentage of local government officials selecting area.

Implications

Several implications arise about the nature of practitioner-oriented training and education in the year 2000. In all likelihood, chief administrative officers of smaller cities will be slightly more eager than officials in larger cities to acquire assistance in enhancing the internal operations of city hall. This may be due to the existing recruitment pattern in both settings. Larger city governments tend to have the resources to attract technical specialists more readily, while smaller settings tend to adapt and "make do" with the recruitment of generalists. The result is that larger city governments have improved their internal administrative skills, perhaps to the detriment of external "political" activities. Conversely, it is quite possible that smaller local governments have demonstrated a capability for dealing with the local environment, but they have neglected the development of an effective internal management capacity.

In a fundamental way, therefore, future training and education must provide a balance in both trends. It must provide a "generalist" expertise in dealing with the external environment for the officials of larger cities, and provide the small-town generalist with technical and specialized expertise that will be needed in the effective and efficient running of local government.

SUMMARY

This chapter has sought to outline current and future training needs of local government practitioners. In general, practitioners perceive that training and assistance are currently required in the following areas: personnel performance, disciplinary practices, community relations, working with elected officials, computer literacy, program evaluation, and merit principles and practices. It is interesting that city managers and mayors identified similar future training and assistance needs, placing the greatest emphasis on the areas of computer literacy, budgeting, community relations, program evaluation/needs assessment, public works/capital financing, and writing and oral communication skills. Although some differences were found in training and assistance needs based on form of government and access to university-based outreach units, the size of the city seemed to have the greatest impact, with smaller cities expressing the greatest needs, and yet clearly having the least amount of resources to meet these needs. These differences, however, tend to be marginal.

Acquiring state-of-the-art training and education for local government personnel is a concern shared by many leaders in the public sector (Poister and Streib, 1989a and 1989b; Slack, 1990), private-sector consulting firms (Ammons and Glass, 1988), and universities (Dunn, Gibson, and Whorton, 1985; Hambrick, 1983). Continual training and education offer a wide variety of opportunities to local government managers, including that of increasing the staff's sense of professionalism (Wiseman, 1989) and its role in the decision-making process (Accordino, 1989), as well as its understanding of the political environment (Lewis and Raffel, 1988).

Even with Clinton's Democratic administration, municipalities will need to continue to search for answers and solutions in sources other than the federal government. Clearly, the message from President Clinton is a change from dependency to self-sufficiency. Municipalities will have to find increased capacity for acquiring additional expertise either from within the ranks of their own work force or from other sources closer to home than Washington.

NOTE

1. Items constituting each scale are as follows:

Scale	Questionnaire item
Information and Library Utilization	Local Government Data Bank
	Legislative Histories
	Local Government Documents / Reports
	"How To" / Model Manuals
	Professional Journals / Books
	Federal / State Government Depository
	Census Data
Maintenance and Operation Needs Assessment	Program Evaluation / Needs
	Contract Management
	Public Works / Capital Financing
	Statistical / Data Analysis
	Computer Literacy

	Grant Proposal Writing and Administration
	Maintenance Functions
Fiscal Concerns	Budgeting
	Accounting
	Cash Management
Human Resource	Equal Employment Opportunity
Management	Writing and Oral Community
	Employee Benefits
	Labor Relations
	Personnel Staffing
	Merit Promotion Principles and Practices
	Disciplinary Practices
	Safety / Health Conditions
	Office and Interoffice Communications and Work
Relations	Position Classification / Wage and Salary Analysis
	Managing Personnel Performance
External Environment	Community Relations
	Working with Elected Officials

Cronbach's Alpha, employed to determine the internal consistency of items constituting each of the five scales, produced acceptable results:

Dimension	Cronbach's Alpha
Information Needs	0.75
Maintenance Needs	0.60
Fiscal Needs	0.71
Human Resource Needs	0.77
External Environment Needs	0.69

Chapter 5

Additional Training and Assistance Needs for the Present and Future

The previous chapter focused on mayoral and city manager perceptions of current and future training, assistance, and information needs. The changing environment in which local government functions, however, places practitioners in a position of having to develop or acquire expertise in several areas other than those covered in the survey of municipal training and assistance needs discussed in Chapter 4. In this chapter, we focus on three additional, specific areas in need of immediate, as well as continued, future attention. While these three areas generally fall under the rubric of human resources management, we expect that the development of expertise in each of these areas will require mayors and city managers to reach beyond current practices in this discipline.

First and foremost, municipal officials must become knowledgeable and skillful at managing an increasingly diverse work force. Given the projected demographic changes and new federal legislation discussed in Chapter 2, city governments must acquire a greater array of skills and expertise in managing more effectively a work force that is becoming increasingly diverse. As the persons with primary responsibility for developing and maintaining a tolerant workplace environment that welcomes and nurtures the diversity of all its employees, mayors and city managers must be able to use training and development experiences to advance this effort.

Related to the area of workplace diversity are issues of maintaining "special populations" in the work force. Because of current and changing demographics, expertise is also needed to make the workplace more conducive to the productivity of employees with disabilities. Thus, a second area of training, assistance, and information in which mayors and city managers will need to develop expertise relates to managing workplaces that accommodate the entry and successful participation of individuals with disabilities. With the passage of the Americans with Disabilities Act (ADA), cities must become familiar with the details of this act to understand how the ADA affects human resources management practices.

Finally, we believe there will be an increasing need for training, assistance, and information regarding managing a work force that includes and respects the rights of employees who have or are at risk for acquiring AIDS. As an increasing number of employees are becoming infected with HIV, cities must develop policies and training experiences to disseminate information on AIDS in the workplace.

EXPERTISE FOR MANAGING DIVERSITY

In the previous chapter, we reported that city managers and mayors do not perceive a great need for training and assistance in the area of affirmative action and equal employment opportunities. The low ranking may be due to the fact that municipalities have had more than two decades, since the passage of the EEOA, to become expert in the area of affirmative-action recruitment and promotion practices. In some instances, low rankings on this issue may also reflect resentment toward programs that appear to be externally driven and result in additional staff time and paperwork.

Differences between affirmative action and diversity are not always clear to either the practitioner or the public. An understanding of the philosophy and practice of affirmative action is necessary for developing sound and legal recruitment and promotion processes. An understanding of diversity is necessary for developing an atmosphere of productivity and retention. While practition-

ers may neither want nor require assistance in the area of affirmative action, the changing demographics of America necessitate that
they acquire expertise for managing diversity in the workplace.

As illustrated in Tables 5.1 through 5.3, the reasons for acquiring
a greater understanding and appreciation of diversity are becoming increasingly apparent. The population of ethnic groups in
America is increasing exponentially, especially among Asians,
Hispanics, and Native Americans. In contrast to their mothers'
and grandmothers' generations, women today constitute a strong
force in society, with increasing numbers working outside the
home. By the year 2005, almost two-thirds of the women in this
country will be found in the workplace and, furthermore, nearly
half of the American work force will be composed of women. Certainly the issue and ramifications of work force diversity will
become increasingly difficult for managers and supervisors to
ignore or view as secondary concerns in their daily routines.

Clearly, concern for managing a more diverse work force is not
merely an issue of quantity, that is, the increased numbers and
percentages of people of color and white women in the workplace.
There is also significant evidence that suggests the municipal government environment will become qualitatively different and
more culturally complex in the near future than it is today. Trends
point toward a new layering of diversity, adding broader issues of
culture and language to the existing challenges of race, ethnicity,

Table 5.1
U.S. Population by Race and Origin, 1980 and 1990

	1980 (in thousands)	1990 (in thousands)	Percentage Change
All Persons	226,546	248,710	9.8
White	188,372	199,686	6.0
Black	26,495	29,986	13.2
Native American	1,420	1,959	37.9
Asian or Pacific Islander	3,500	7,274	107.8
Hispanic	14,609	22,354	53.0
Other	6,758	9,805	45.1

Source: U.S. Bureau of the Census, press release CB91-216.

Table 5.2
U.S. Population by Gender, Selected Years

	Total Population (in thousands)	Percentage Women
1940	137,670	47.7
1950	151,326	50.0
1970	203,235	51.0
1990	248,710	51.3

Sources: U.S. Bureau of the Census, U.S. Census of Population: 1940, vol. II, part 1; 1950, vol. II, part 1; 1970, vol. I, part B; Current Population Reports, series P-25, No. 1045.

and gender. The emergence of this new layering can be seen from several developments.

First, there seems to be a renaissance among all ethnic groups in America. The growing number and popularity of ethnic celebrations in every major municipality is indicative of this renewal, as is the reverse migration of young suburbanites who now wish to experience urban life much as their grandparents did. It is also evi-

Table 5.3
Women and the American Workplace, Selected Years

	Percentage of Women Working Outside the Home	Percentage of Women as Part of the Total Work Force
1940	28.2	25.5
1950	33.1	29.6
1960	36.1	32.2
1970	43.3	38.0
1980	51.5	42.6
1990	57.5	45.4
2000	62.0	46.9
2005	63.0	47.4

Sources: U.S. Bureau of the Census, Statistical Abstract of the United States: 1992 (p. 381, Table 609); 1965 (p. 217, Table 298); 1960 (p. 205, Table 263), Washington, D.C.

denced by the revitalization of many of the ethnic neighborhoods, like Cleveland's "Little Italy" and "Slavic Village." Where once "old world" traditions were the concern of only the elderly and first-generation Americans, those same values and practices are rapidly becoming important to postwar baby boomers and their children. As complexity in the postindustrial city engulfs its inhabitants (Pohlmann, 1993), there will be a corresponding search for themes and traditions that people hope will help them make a little more sense out of their lives. In addition to religion, therefore, a greater appreciation of cultural and ethnic heritage seems to be offering many people much-needed comfort and understanding.

Second, the layering of diversity is aided by the growing number of immigrants to the United States. Not since the turn of the twentieth century have so many people come to the United States to live and work. Table 5.4 compares the admission rates of immigrants for the years 1980 and 1990. Table 5.5 reports the numbers of new Americans and rate of immigration for the last three decades. We have every reason to assume that this trend will continue and that employees in city government, as well as all other sectors of the economy, can expect to have more opportunities for interaction with new and foreign-born Americans.

Finally, in addition to issues of managing a diverse work force, developments along the U.S. border, as well as increased interdependence across these borders, also have the potential of contributing additional layers of diversity to the municipal government work environment. An increase in interactions with Canadians and

Table 5.4
Immigration to the United States, 1980, 1985, and 1990

	Number of Immigrants	*Rate**
1980	530,639	2.3
1985	601,516	2.4
1990	1,536,483	6.1

Source: U.S. Immigration and Naturalization Service, Statistical Yearbook, 1980, 1985, 1990, Washington, D.C.

*Per 1,000 population. Rate computed by dividing immigration by U.S. population.

Table 5.5
Immigration to the United States, 1960 to 1989, by Decade

	Number of Immigrants	_Rate*_
1960-69	3,322,000	1.7
1970-79	4,493,000	2.1
1980-89	7,338,000	3.1

Source: U.S. Immigration and Naturalization Service. Statistical Yearbook, 1980, 1985, 1990, Washington, D.C.

*Per 1,000 population. Rate computed by dividing sum of annual immigration totals by sum of annual U.S. population totals for same number of years.

Mexicans, for instance, might well introduce a linguistic dimension into the equation. Americans sometimes overlook the differences in language and customs of people who live within short driving distance of their northern and southern borders. This is a bit surprising, given that there are over 7 million French-speaking Canadians on the other side of New York and the upper New England border and approximately 13 million Spanish-speaking Mexicans who live near the southwestern part of the United States.

While a strong interrelationship has always existed between the United States and Canada, the effects of having French-speaking people across the border remain somewhat dormant. Quebec is the most independent-minded province in Canada and, therefore, tries to maintain a posture of being the least reliant on relations with the United States (Nelles, 1990). The border area of upper New England, especially Maine, while populated by many French-Americans, is quite parochial in nature. Towns located there show little concern for establishing economic or policy ties with their counterpart communities in Quebec (Nelles, 1990). These two situations, Quebec self-reliance and New England parochialism, could easily change in the next decade or so. Therefore, local governments in this region may have to prepare for dealing effectively with many new cultural ramifications resulting from closer ties with French-speaking Canada.

In contrast, the ramifications of additional cultural and linguistic diversity are becoming more pronounced throughout the southwestern part of the United States. As illustrated in Table 5.6, one of the primary developments in this region is a rapidly expanding population. Nearly one of every five Americans, as well as 15 percent of all Mexicans, live in states along the border. Expanding populations on both sides of the border, in conjunction with international agreements like the North American Free Trade Agreement (NAFTA), mean that more people will have greater access to each nation's local markets.

Perhaps an even more important development is the change in the psychology of this region. In the minds of both citizens and governments, the U.S.-Mexican geo-political border is rapidly being overshadowed by the realization of interdependency of economies, politics, and public policies. The quality of air in El Paso, Texas, for instance, is directly dependent on auto emission standards in Cuidad Juarez. The burden of financing education in the Deming, New Mexico, school system is affected by the number of Mexican children who slip across the border each day to attend

Table 5.6
Population in Border States, United States and Mexico

	1980 (in thousands)	1990 (in thousands)	Percentage Change
U.S. States	**42,004.4**	**52,211.7**	**18.23**
Arizona	2,735.6	3,681.4	34.57
California	23,796.8	29,955.7	25.88
New Mexico	1,310.3	1,519.6	15.97
Texas	14,161.7	17,055.0	18.94
Mexican States	**10,691.9**	**13,222.2**	**23.67**
Baja California	1,177.9	1,657.9	40.75
Chihuahua	2,005.5	2,440.0	21.66
Coahuila	1,557.3	1,971.3	26.59
Nuevo Leon	2,513.0	3,086.5	22.82
Sonora	1,513.7	1,822.3	20.38
Tamaulipas	1,924.5	2,244.2	16.61

Sources: U.S. Department of Commerce, Bureau of Economic Analysis, Machine Readable Data Files; Instituto Nacional de Geografia y Informaca, *X Censo General de Poblacion y Vivienda, 1980*, *XI Censo de Poblacin y Vivienda, 1990*, various volumes (Secretaria de programmacion y Presupuesto, Mexico, D.F.). With the assistance of the Center for Latin American Studies, New Mexico State University.

classes there because they are unable to obtain adequate schooling in Palomas, Chihuahua. The level of pollution in the Rio Grande as it flows through the state of Nuevo Leon is affected greatly by contaminants entering the river upstream in Santa Fe and Albuquerque. The increasing awareness of interdependence in areas of both strengths and weakness is quietly galvanizing this area into a unique cultural region of over 55 million people.

This new layering of diversity clearly will add complexity to our needs for diversity training. On the one hand, increasing percentages of women and people of color within the work force suggest a need for new managerial tools and human relations skills to assist in the balancing of two very different and difficult tasks. First, supervisors must learn to be color- (with regard to race and ethnicity) and gender-blind. Throughout the daily routine of work, employees must be treated equally as individuals, without taking into consideration race, ethnicity, or gender. This task requires attention to standard training for managers in the areas of human resource management, leadership skills, merit assessment and performance appraisal, and team-building.

At the same time, supervisors must also develop a "mindfulness" (Gudykunst, 1991) about the unique and varied strengths and challenges that people of color and white women bring to the workplace. After all, these strengths and challenges are integral to developing "passive representation" (Mosher, 1968) within the public service. Women and people of different racial, ethnic, and cultural backgrounds provide specialized and much-needed additional information, not just about the people who work in city hall, but also about the people being served by city government. This suggests that both in terms of the effects on internal operations and in the delivery of programs, race- and gender-based differences among employees must be understood and appreciated by all members of the work force. This requires training in sensitivity toward diversity.

In addition, whether as a result of a renewed interest in ethnic group identification, the arrival of new immigrant Americans, or the development of closer ties with Mexicans and French-Canadians, new layers of diversity are being added to the environment of local government. Throughout the United States, municipalities will deliver services to a public increasingly characterized by having a heightened sensitivity toward ethnicity. The growing awareness of interdependency along the border area will also place a special burden on local governments throughout California, Arizona, New Mexico, and Texas. To solve mutual problems, as well as to capitalize on common strengths, local government practitioners will find it necessary to work effectively with their counterparts across the border. City managers and mayors must not only equip their organizations with the expertise to appreciate foreign cultures, but they will also need to develop the capacity to communicate much more frequently in a foreign language.

EXPERTISE FOR MANAGING EMPLOYEES WITH DISABILITIES

Title I of the Americans with Disabilities Act underscores the workplace rights of persons with disabilities. Decisions about recruitment, hiring, retention, and promotion must be taken without regard to the specific impairment of a protected disabled individual, as long as that person is otherwise qualified to perform the essential functions of the position and can do so with or without the aid of reasonable accommodations that limit or nullify the job-related effects of the impairment. First-line managers, as well as chief administrative officers, must develop a firm working knowledge of every component of the legislation. Acquiring such expertise, however, can be problematic due to the desire of Congress to permit the greatest degree of discretion in the application of ADA at each worksite. Consequences of such flexibility for managers and supervisors can be seen in at least three key terms used in the legislation: reasonable accommodation, undue hardship, and the designation of being "otherwise qualified."

Two of the primary questions currently being asked by practitioners are: What is "reasonable accommodation"?; and How do I apply it to my own worksite? While Section 101(9) (B) of the ADA includes examples of possible categories of acceptable activities,[1] and Equal Employment Opportunity Commission (EEOC) regulations provide some guidance in developing acceptable options,[2] practitioners will be pressed to find either a concise definition of the term or a comprehensive list of acceptable strategies to provide such accommodations for disabled employees and job applicants. As is illustrated by the following exchange between Senators Orrin

Hatch (R-Utah) and Tom Harkin (D-Iowa) (*Congressional Record*, S10735, September 7, 1989), this was the intent of Congress.

> *Mr. Hatch*: It is my understanding that a reasonable accommodation . . . would take into consideration the nature of a particular industry for the purpose of determining what type of accommodation would or would not, constitute an undue hardship. In other words, the Americans with Disabilities Act would not require that a specific accommodation, which could be easily made in a traditional office setting, be implemented in a nontraditional setting, such as construction worksite, if it imposed an undue hardship. Would my colleague please comment on whether or not my interpretation of the language and intent of this legislation is correct, with regard to different industries employing different types of accommodation.

> *Mr. Harkin*: I would say to my friend from Utah that he has correctly interpreted the "reasonable accommodation" requirement of Title I of the ADA bill. Just as each person with a disability is unique in his or her requirements for accommodation to help meet their potential in the workplace, each industry, indeed each separate business, may be unique in the type of accommodation employers are able to provide without significant difficulty or expense.

The same degree of ambiguity is found in making the initial determination of whether or not a request of a specific accommodation is actually "reasonable." In Section 101(10) (B) of the legislation, practitioners will find only very general criteria for establishing what accommodations represent "undue hardship":

- the nature and cost of the specific accommodation
- the nature and circumstance of the specific worksite
- the nature and circumstance of the entire organization (beyond the specific department or worksite)
- the type of operation of the worksite.

Mayors and city managers will also be hard-pressed to find a concise description of what constitutes an "otherwise qualified" disabled job applicant or employee. The legislation places the determination of who is "otherwise qualified" under the rubric of the essential functions of each job. Practitioners will have to either develop or reexamine the job descriptions of all positions within the municipal workplace and ensure that descriptions of the essential and marginal functions of each position are clear.

Legislative flexibility ostensibly offers many options to the practitioner. But in the case of the ADA, the extent of discretion actually places a greater burden on the practitioner, who must make the initial attempt at defining much of the ADA, as well as formulate strategies for its implementation—within the context of the particular worksite and within the framework of the individual qualities of each disabled job applicant or employee. In addition to understanding the law, the practitioner must acquire a deeper appreciation of the mechanics of each position within the organization, the nature of each worksite, the resource capacity of the municipality, and the nature and workplace consequences of specific impairments of qualified disabled employees and job applicants. Ultimately, city managers and mayors will be held accountable, by both the judicial system and the citizenry, for acquiring and using the expertise needed for managing a workplace conducive to disabled Americans.

EXPERTISE FOR MANAGING AIDS IN THE WORKPLACE

AIDS is rapidly becoming the most pressing health issue in America, as well as one of the most pressing issues facing the American workplace. Of the more than 300,000 people in the United States who have contracted AIDS, 98 percent are between 20 and 65 years of age and approximately 80 percent are in the prime working ages of 24 to 40 (U.S. Department of Health and Human Services, July 1993). Equally disturbing, AIDS is the leading cause of death among women between the ages of 20 and 44 in urban areas throughout North America (U.S. Department of Health and Human Services, February 1991). Currently, about 2.5 million Americans are infected with HIV, the virus that causes

AIDS (Slack, 1991). Most of these people, unaware of their condition, are also in the midst of their most productive years. AIDS is draining the health and productivity of the work force.

Government must deal with the issue of AIDS and the workplace, especially if it expects the private sector to do the same. Local government must be particularly prepared to address the workplace ramifications of this epidemic because, as reported in Chapter 1, the local government workplace is the single largest focal point of employment in the United States. Yet in the second decade (since the mid-1970s) of this crisis, many governmental units are ill-prepared to deal with the consequences of AIDS. This is especially the case outside the national government, where readiness to handle a variety of AIDS-related tasks "varies considerably among states and cities" (Johnson and Jones, 1991). Moreover, a recent study of local government preparedness found that only 10 percent of municipalities have a plan to deal with AIDS in their own work setting (Slack, 1991). The same study discovered that city managers and mayors tend to underestimate, by a magnitude of six, the number of HIV-infected people working for them.

These two factors, unpreparedness and underestimating the impact of the epidemic, spell disaster for the public workplace. Consequences include unexpected increases in health care costs and sick-day utilization, co-worker misunderstanding, recruitment and training of replacement personnel, law suits, and an incremental, yet substantial, loss in productivity. The assessment made by James A. Johnson and Walter J. Jones (1991) of the need for responsiveness of public health officials seems applicable to local government's readiness to deal with the disease in its own workplace. No other crisis in the 1990s will loom more ominously than AIDS. Regrettably, this crisis is bound to carry over well into the twenty-first century.

Why Should Local Government Have an AIDS Plan?

There are three reasons that employers should institute a plan for managing the workplace ramifications of AIDS. First, there is a moral imperative. Good management recognizes the *quid pro quo* it enjoys with the work force. Employees are expected to "come through" for management, while management is expected to "take care" of its employees. Management's part of the bargain, typically manifested through employee assistance programs, must expand to address the AIDS crisis. Management should have a plan of action to assist workers in the HIV spectrum, just as it has adopted activities to help employees deal with other problems.

Second, an AIDS plan can help management comply with the law. The Americans with Disabilities Act regards people with HIV as disabled individuals and therefore prohibits discriminatory employment practices against people with HIV and requires employers to provide "reasonable accommodations" for these workers so that they may perform the essential functions of their jobs. As discussed above, mayors and city managers will be held accountable for acquiring and using the expertise needed to manage a workplace conducive to individuals with disabilities. An AIDS plan can act as a reminder of both the employee's civil rights and employer's legal obligations.

Third, an AIDS plan can help management control workplace-related costs of AIDS and maintain current levels of productivity. As discussed in Chapter 2, there is no doubt that AIDS is an expensive disease. While an effective AIDS plan cannot eliminate these costs, it can help managers use more wisely both material and human resources. Knowing how to provide reasonable accommodation, for instance, can keep workers with HIV healthier for longer periods of time. Doing so will postpone the use of expensive health care packages, as well as the incumbent cost and effort of replacing personnel. Knowing how to manage the fears and prejudices of co-workers and managers can help reduce the omnipresent threat of lawsuit.

A Model AIDS Plan for the Workplace

To examine this area of training and assistance need, AIDS-related plans and documents were collected from ninety-seven cities and counties throughout the United States.[3] These plans were analyzed with regard to what we believe are the four essential components of an AIDS-in-the-workplace plan (Slack, 1991):

1. A statement of organizational support for the workplace rights of all seropositive (HIV) employees and prospective employees

2. A set of procedures to be followed when dealing with seropositive employees

3. A set of workplace-related services available to seropositive employees

4. A plan for providing education to all employees, as well as continual training to supervisors on managing AIDS-related situations in the workplace

Here we present examples of statements from the collected documents to demonstrate how cities might develop an effective AIDS-in-the-workplace plan.

Component 1. A Statement of Organizational Support for the Workplace Rights of All Seropositive (HIV) Employees and Prospective Employees.

This component reaffirms management's commitment to implementing ADA guidelines in the workplace. Existing AIDS plans incorporate language regarding the civil rights of seropositive workers.

Honolulu, Hawaii

The City recognizes that some of its employees may have or may contract an infectious/contagious disease, and that some of its prospective employees may have such diseases. It is the City's policy that employees and prospective employees shall not be discriminated against in employment because they have such diseases, provided they are able to perform their jobs in a satisfactory manner without undue hazard to themselves or others.

Pierce County, Washington

It is the policy of Pierce County to preserve the right to equal employment opportunity for all persons including those with physical, mental or sensory disabilities. Acquired Immunodeficiency Syndrome and other AIDS virus-related conditions are considered to be disabilities protected by Washington State law and Federal law. Pierce County is also committed to providing a healthy work environment for all County employees.

Sanford, Florida

Any person with AIDS, ARC, or HIV shall have every protection made available to handicapped persons.

Component 2: A Set of Procedures to Be Followed When Dealing with Seropositive Employees.

This component protects the employer from law suit. First, it should remind supervisors of the need to maintain strict confidentiality in dealing with employee health matters.

Los Angeles, California

[Management's actions] must reflect sensitivity to the specially confidential nature of HIV-related information. The law has very strict requirements regarding the circumstances under which disclosure of such information may occur because of AIDS' powerful potential for social stigma.

Tucson, Arizona

A person's physical or mental condition is personal and confidential. City employees who have access to an applicant's or employee's medical record are to maintain that individual's privacy, and take reasonable precautions to prevent unnecessary distribution of such information.

This component should also address the fears and possible actions of co-workers.

Newark, California

Supervisors need to be sensitive and responsive to co-workers' concerns and fears about life-threatening illnesses.

Farmington, Connecticut

Since the Town of Farmington maintains a policy of providing a work environment free of discrimination and harassment, Department Heads and Supervisors will take whatever steps are necessary to stem slurs of employees based upon actual OR PERCEIVED presence of HIV, or actual OR PERCEIVED presence of AIDS diagnosis in their employees. Supervisors are responsible for compliance and communication of the non-discrimination and non-harassment policy. Violations of the policy will be grounds for disciplinary action, including discharge if necessary.

St. Joseph, Missouri

Supervisors need to be encouraged to confront workplace rumors. Disciplinary action will be taken against anyone who attempts to spread rumors about, or isolate or harass, the employee with AIDS.

San Marcos, Texas

Refusal to work with an employee or to provide services to anyone who has been diagnosed as having a life-threatening illness shall be cause for disciplinary action.

*Component 3: A Set of Workplace-Related Services
Available to Seropositive Employees.*

In this component, management affirms its commitment to providing reasonable accommodation to seropositive workers. The ADA permits discretion in defining reasonable accommodations so that the nature of the worksite and the resources of the organization can be taken into account. Reasonable accommodations for seropositive employees may include flextime, job restructuring, job transfers, modems and computer equipment for use at home, health care benefits, and life insurance consultation. It is in this section that management specifies what services and accommodations are available.

Portsmouth, Virginia

Supervisors of employees who are diagnosed with life-threatening diseases shall make reasonable accommodations to allow employees to continue working: this may include, among other things, changes in the physical work environment, adjustment of job duties, or transfer to a more suitable position. Personnel and Health Department staff are available to assist supervisors. Benefits consultation including, but not limited to, health insurance, retirement, leave, and compensation will be provided.

Mt. Pleasant, Michigan

Job modification or transfers may be enacted: to ensure that the AIDS-infected employee is medically fit and able to perform work and work-related tasks; or to avoid exposure of other workers to secondary illnesses which may be contagious.

Fairfax, Virginia

The City will provide reasonable accommodations where possible for employees with life-threatening infectious diseases in order to facilitate the continuance of their employment, which may include, among other things, change in physical environment, adjustment of job duties or transfer to a more suitable position. Each case, however, will be reviewed separately and "reasonable accommodation" must be approved by both the Department Head and City Manager.

This component should also specify services available within the community.

Tempe, Arizona

Human Resources shall provide referral to appropriate community agencies and organizations that offer services for catastrophic illnesses.

Rock County, Wisconsin

An Inmate/Patient/Employee with HIV or AIDS should be encouraged to seek assistance from established community support groups for medical and counseling services. Information can be obtained through M.A.S.N. (Madison AIDS Support Network), (603) 255-1711, or the Rock County Health Department at 755-2640.

Montgomery County, Maryland

General Information and Testing—Montgomery County Department of Health, 593-8507. State AIDS Hotline by HERO (Health Education Resource Organization) for [information and referral], 1-800-638-6252. National Hotline for AIDS is 1-800-342-AIDS.

Component 4: A Plan for Providing Education to All Employees, as Well as Continual Training to Supervisors on Managing AIDS-related Situations in the Workplace.

Education is instrumental in addressing fears about HIV-infection and, subsequently, dispelling rumors about what is unknown about specific workers presumed to be HIV-positive. While all ninety-six AIDS policies provide some sort of basic information to employees, none provides continual training for supervisors.

North Las Vegas, Nevada

The City will sponsor and participate in ongoing AIDS education and awareness seminars. Informational materials may be obtained from the Clark County Health Department.

Prince George's County, Maryland

All County employees are encouraged to receive training on AIDS. AIDS training is provided by the Office of Personnel's Training Institute; each agency's training coordinator will assist employees in scheduling training in this area. Appointing authorities shall insure that a representative number of their employees receive training each year.

Kinston, North Carolina

The City of Kinston shall provide mandatory training and appropriate educational materials concerning AIDS, AIDS-related conditions and a copy of this policy in an orderly and timely manner.

An addendum that delineates and defines all AIDS-related terms should also be included. So that every employee gains in understanding, it is important that these rather complex medical terms be explained as simply as possible.

Chapel Hill, North Carolina

HIV: The Human Immunodeficiency Virus, or HIV. The HIV damages the immune system, the body's defense against disease. The virus may be present in the blood stream for several years before a person develops serious symptoms or becomes sick. Once infected with HIV, a person can pass the virus on to others, even if the infected person looks and feels healthy.

ARC: AIDS Related Complex, in which a person has symptoms of infections which are usually less severe than the infections and cancers present in a person with AIDS.

AIDS: The Acquired Immune Deficiency Syndrome, a serious (and, to date, fatal) illness that harms the body's disease-fighting immune system. Even though a person has the HIV in the bloodstream, he or she is not diagnosed as having AIDS until he or she additionally develops one of several cancers or infections that are usually rare or mild in healthy and uninfected people.

Manchester, New Hampshire

Acquired Immune Deficiency Syndrome (AIDS) is caused by a virus called the human immunodeficiency virus (HIV). This virus can damage the brain and weaken the immune system—allowing a person to become susceptible to certain diseases that healthy individuals would not get (Kaposi's sarcoma, Pneumocystic carinii pneumonia, and others). When a person has one of these opportunistic diseases and is infected by the human immunodeficiency virus, the person is considered to have AIDS. AIDS is the final stage of HIV infection. A person with HIV infection may not develop any symptoms of AIDS for up to 7 or 8 years.

These individuals may look and feel well and may not know that they are infected or carry the AIDS virus. However, once infected, they will remain infected for life.

Implications

A review of these documents provides two lessons about the nature and level of local government's capacity to manage AIDS in its own workplace. First, there appears to be a substantial amount of variation in format and content among the existing AIDS policies. The length of these documents ranges from a few paragraphs (Orem, Utah and Lombard, Illinois) to hundreds of pages (New York and Cleveland). Variation in content ranges from an exclusive focus on AIDS (Upper Merion Township, Pennsylvania), to incorporating AIDS in a larger policy about communicable diseases (Shelby County, Tennessee), to generic statements about keeping workplaces free from discrimination (Seattle, Washington).

The vast majority of documents do not give equal attention to the four components we consider necessary for an AIDS plan. In particular, most local governments neglect to address adequately the education and training needs of the work force. While basic AIDS information is prevalent, too often it is provided either through non-mandatory courses or through distribution of posters and brochures.[4] Local governments simply tend to fail to provide adequate, ongoing training for supervisors on managing AIDS-related situations. Consequently, managers lack explicit opportunities to gain better perspectives of "reasonable accommodation" issues, as well as to learn new techniques on managing the workplace environment in the age of AIDS.

The extent of variation among AIDS plans suggests local governments are "reinventing the wheel" in order to cope with AIDS in the workplace. Predictably, some local governments are more successful than others in finding solutions to workplace problems. Variation in the nature and content of AIDS plans results in sharp discrepancies in the level and quality of preparedness.

The second lesson stems from the existence of only a handful of AIDS documents. The fact that a very limited number of local governments have adopted AIDS plans for their workplaces means that the vast majority of municipalities and counties lack even a minimum level of readiness to cope with this disease. This is regrettable because every employer in the public and private sectors can expect to experience declining health and productivity within the work force as a result of AIDS. Left unprepared, the vast majority of local governments will spend greater levels of money, at a quicker pace, on personnel and health care items. In all likelihood, they will also have to invest many resources in court-room battles with a legal profession that sees more and more of its future in monitoring workplaces.

The importance of a plan to manage workplace ramifications of AIDS cannot be underestimated. Similar to the AA/EEO policy, an AIDS plan helps set the tone within the organization. Its existence draws the attention of both supervisors and employees to the ground rules: what is appropriate conduct, as well as what procedures and services are available. Its acceptance can transform a reactive and hostile workplace into one that is proactive and compassionate in its efforts to minimize AIDS-related costs and maximize productivity in all employees.

CONCLUSIONS

This chapter has focused on three areas that are emerging as key issues for managers in both the public and private sectors: managing diversity, managing employees with disabilities, and managing AIDS in the workplace. These three areas present mayors and city managers with new challenges for developing appropriate expertise within local government. Even more than previously suspected (Slack, 1990; Whorton, Gibson, and Dunn, 1986), providers of practitioner education, training, and assistance may have to redesign and customize their programs and curricula to ensure that future offerings are congruent with the actual needs of, and realities facing, municipal government.

While preparing for these new challenges does not necessarily call for the acquisition of a set of managerial tools completely different from those discussed in Chapter 4, it does call for new approaches, new knowledge and information, and new creativity in refining and enhancing those tools already acquired. To the extent that city governments have begun to move from a singular focus on affirmative action/equal employment opportunity issues to a broader focus on valuing diversity in the work force and developing greater sensitivity in working with people of different gender and races, they can continue to extend this focus to deal with the new layers of workforce diversity. Such an approach to managing diversity will also facilitate an understanding of how employees' different racial, ethnic, and cultural backgrounds can enhance work productivity and may even encourage the learning of Spanish or French. Similarly, gearing up to manage a workplace in the age of AIDS will entail applying new expertise in the ADA and information about the disease, as well as providing managers with resources to accommodate employees who find themselves within the HIV spectrum and skills to help address fears and possible actions of other employees.

Given the uncertain and potentially turbulent environmental changes taking place, perhaps only one thing is certain about managing the municipal workplace of the twenty-first century. It will become increasingly important to anticipate the types of skills and expertise that may be needed within the unique characteristics of each setting. We are convinced that it is in the best interest of local government to acquire the necessary managerial tools before having them becomes essential to complying with the law, avoiding costly litigation, maintaining high productivity and morale, and providing compassion to both employees and citizens.

NOTES

1. For example,
   - job restructuring
   - part-time or modified work schedules
   - reassignment to a vacant position
   - acquisition or modification of equipment or devices
   - appropriate adjustment or modification of examinations, training materials, or policies
   - providing of qualified readers or interpreters.

2. 56 Fed. Reg. 35,744 (July 26, 1991):
   - Any modification or adjustment to a job application process that enables a qualified individual with a disability to be considered for the position such qualified individual desires
   - Any modification or adjustment to the work environment, or the manner or circumstances under which the position held or desired is customarily performed, that enables a qualified individual with a disability to perform the essential functions of that position

- Any modification or adjustment that enables a covered entity's employee with a disability to enjoy equal (not necessarily the same) benefits and privileges of employment as are enjoyed by its other similarly situated employees without disabilities.

3. Out of a list of 166 local governments provided by the International City Management Association, the following governmental units provided documentation:

Alexandria, VA	Milpatas, CA
Anchorage, AK	Minneapolis, MN
Athens, OH	Montgomery Co., MD
Beaverton, OR	Morris Co., NJ
Bellevue, WA	Mt. Pleasant, MI
Benton Co., MN	Muskegon Co., MI
Bloomington, IL	Newark, CA
Brown Co., MN	New York, NY
Brunswick Co., NC	Nicollet Co., MN
Carver Co., MN	Northeast Ohio Sewer Dist., OH
Centre Co., PA	North Las Vegas, NV
Chambersburg, PA	Oklahoma City, OK
Chapel Hill, NC	Orem, UT
Chippewa Co., WS	Palo Alto, CA
Clallam Co., WA	Phoenix, AZ
Clark Co., NV	Pierce Co., WA
Cleveland, OH	Pinellas Co., FL
Cole Co., MO	Polk Co., MN
Eau Clair, WS	Portsmouth, VA
Edmond, OK	Prince George's Co., MD
Escondido, CA	Puyallup, WA
Fairfax, VA	Redmond, WA
Farmington, CT	Richmond, VA
Fauquier Co., VA	Rock Co., WI
Grand Haven, MI	Rocky Hill, CT
Greenville, TX	Roseburg, OR
Jackson Co., OR	San Carlos, CA
Jacksonville, FL	Sandy City, UT
Jefferson Co., KY	Sanford, FL
Henrico Co., VA	San Marcos, CA
Honolulu, HI	San Marcos, TX
Irving, TX	Santee, CA
Isabella Co., MI	Scott Co., MN
Itasca Co., MN	Seattle, WA
King Co., WA	Shelby Co., TN
Kinston, NC	Sierra Vista, AZ
Kirkland, VA	St. Joseph, MO

Laguna Beach, CA
Lancaster Co., NE
Lenawee Co., MI
Lincoln, NE
Logan Co., OH
Lombard, IL
Lompoc, CA
Lorain Co., OH
Los Angeles, CA
Manchester, NH
Mesa, AZ
Midland, TX

St. Mary's Co., MD
Stearns Co., MN
Tempe, AZ
Tucson, AZ
Upper Merion Township, PA
Vermillion, SD
Wake Co., NC
Westerville, OH
West St. Paul, MN
Wichita, KS
Woodridge, IL

4. It is unfortunate that municipalities and counties do not take advantage of the best source of information on AIDS, the Gay Men's Health Crisis (GMHC). This is the oldest and most experienced counseling center in the United States. GMHC can answer questions about all aspects of the AIDS crisis, from modes of transmission and safer-sex practices to legalities of HIV antibody blood testing in the workplace. It can also provide information about AIDS organizations in every community. GMHC can be reached at (212) 807-6655.

Chapter 6

Preparing Municipalities for the Twenty-First Century

About at the turn of this century, then-Professor Woodrow Wilson made the argument that the public service must become:

> the instrument of humanity, of social betterment. Its business is to establish and maintain every condition which will assist the people to a sound and wholesome and successful life. (1984)

Wilson was speaking during a time of great challenge to the American public service. Events and trends of his day necessitated fundamental changes in the definition and performance of the bureaucratic function. One set of ramifications for public administration education and training, arising out of the new challenges, was a re-exploration of both paradigm and purpose.

As we approach the turn of the twenty-first century, the public service is entering another era of great challenge. The challenges at this point, however, are multiple and much more complex than those of Wilson's time. They involve dealing effectively, legally, and compassionately with a host of issues pertaining to the demand for increased organizational responsibilities, the need for greater workplace performance, and the reality of growing workforce diversity.

Difficulties in meeting these challenges are compounded by three dimensions of the local government environment. Decision-making is heavily influenced by more than a decade of budget cutbacks and reductions-in-force, resulting in the so-called "hollowing" (Lan and Rosenbloom, 1992) of the public service. There is constant competition with an invigorated private sector for the employment of top applicants. Typically, there is also an absence of information about, and acquisition of, the latest conceptual, methodological, and technological advances in the art and science of management.

Customary patterns of response, involving the application of managerial and analytical principles grounded firmly in nineteenth-century public administration experiences and thought, can neither explain nor remedy the complex array of new crises, situations, and issues that are rapidly unfolding. As in the time of Wilson, there are implications for public administration training, education, and assistance. For the public service to remain a viable "instrument of humanity," especially at the municipal level, we must find more effective strategies to equip current and future managers with the intellectual tools and understanding needed to address successfully the complex challenges that lie before them.

This book has focused on the training, education, and assistance needs of municipal governments as they prepare to face the challenges of the twenty-first century. Our arguments and findings are fairly straightforward. An investment in training represents a commitment to the future of the municipal organization as well as the community itself. A successful training program requires the utilization of a systems approach. Organizational and employee needs must be accurately assessed. Based on that assessment, a training program must be adequately designed and implemented. Equally important, although often neglected, is an evaluation component, which must be incorporated to measure short-term results and long-term consequences of the training program.

Based on survey research, we find that the perceived training and assistance needs of city managers and mayors are quite varied and complex. Currently, the greatest needs are found in the areas of developing sound personnel performance systems, understanding and implementing the principles of merit, creating fair and effective disciplinary practices, and building sound relations with citizens and elected officials of the community. By the turn of the twenty-first century, municipal government practitioners also anticipate need for training and assistance in the areas of writing and oral communications, public works and capital finance, computer literacy, budgeting, and program evaluation.

Respondents in this survey indicate basically similar training and assistance needs regardless of whether the community has adopted a council-manager or mayor-council form of municipal government. For the most part, however, city managers and mayors from smaller communities tend to recognize the need for training and assistance at slightly higher levels than do their counterparts in larger cities. Regardless of background factors, the major trend in perceived future training and assistance needs shifts attention from the acquisition of interpersonal skills toward more of the "nuts and bolts" and "how-to" kinds of information. This is perhaps reflective of a quiet desperation on the part of city managers and mayors—something that has gradually evolved from the budgetary and political realities of having to find effective ways of doing more with less in both the delivery of services and the operation of city hall.

Along with the perceived needs of local government practitioners, we believe that training and assistance will be necessary to deal with the additional layering of diversity that is rapidly developing within the work force. Supervisors will have to manage work units that are increasingly characterized by members of a host of ethnic, religious, and cultural groups, as well as women and people of color. Similarly, employees will have to accept the authority of supervisors who have circumvented the "glass ceiling" (Bullard and Wright, 1993) and are members of these diverse groups. Because the Americans with Disabilities Act leaves little room for local manipulation (Bishop and Jones, 1993), the workplace will have no choice but to learn to accommodate disabled Americans. This will include people infected with human immunodeficiency virus and AIDS.

Contrary to the perceived needs of local government practitioners, managing the additional ramifications of these new layers of diversity in the workplace will require more interpersonal skills and sensitivity training. Contrary to the perceived needs of city

managers and mayors, effectiveness in human resource management will necessitate more, not less, training and assistance in
understanding and applying the nuances of future federal requirements for equal employment opportunity and affirmative action,
which will certainly be a function of the added layers of diversity.

RECOMMENDATIONS FOR IMPROVING THE ROLE OF TRAINING

As pointed out in Chapter 2, local governments allocate less
than 1 percent of their operating budgets to training and the
acquisition of information and assistance. If an investment in
training is a commitment to the future, it is appropriate to ask how
the importance of this function can be increased to meet current
and future challenges of municipal government.

We have three recommendations.

First, municipal officials must be given a better idea of the kinds
of training that are available and, equally important, where the
expertise can be found either to conduct the training sessions for
the targeted staff or to train as trainers a smaller group of municipal employees. Some examples can be found in Appendix B.
These are categorized by: (1) personnel-related training, such as
on the Americans with Disabilities Act and the workplace ramifications of AIDS; (2) workplace operations-related training, such as
grant-writing and public works; (3) program-related training,
such as program evaluation and neighborhood block analysis; and
(4) external relations training modules, such as working with the
media and public leadership training.

Second, we suggest that universities be encouraged to become
more involved with providing training and assistance to local
governments. Our findings indicate that about half of the municipalities in the survey have never been contacted by a university
about training and education opportunities. This observation is
somewhat unsettling because 93 percent of the communities in
this sample were located within a fifty-mile radius, and 98 percent
were located within a one-hundred-mile radius, of a university.

Table 6.1 suggests that university training units tend to focus
more on local governments in larger communities than they do on
those found in smaller communities. This trend is also quite dis-

Table 6.1
Municipalities and University-Based Outreach Units

	Percentage of Larger Communities	Percentage of Smaller Communities
Contact by University	61	38
50-mile radius from university	96	90
100-mile radius from university	100	97

Source: Compiled by the author.

turbing because our findings in Chapter 4 suggest that smaller municipalities have a slightly greater need for training and assistance than do their larger counterparts. It is equally disturbing because distances between larger communities and universities are not significantly different from distances between those same universities and smaller communities. For whatever reasons—the need for profitability in training programs, the prerequisite of a critical mass of trainees or workshop participants, or the resultant prestige of serving the larger cities and communities of the state— it appears that smaller municipalities, and their training and assistance needs, are being ignored by those units providing outreach services at universities.

The obligations of public universities extend far beyond that of simply subsidizing the education of traditional, pre-service students. State-assisted universities also have a responsibility to assist taxpayers and their communities regardless of size and location. This is especially true in the case of the fifty land-grant universities throughout the nation. These institutions of higher education were founded on the premise that providing assistance to communities and regions throughout their respective states is essential to their mission.

There are several good models of university involvement in training and assistance throughout the United States. Two are highlighted in Tables 6.2 and 6.3. The University of Georgia, in Athens, Georgia, is perhaps foremost of the land-grant universities in providing comprehensive training opportunities to municipalities. The Center for Government Research and Public Service at Bowling Green State University, Bowling Green, Ohio, is an

Table 6.2
Governmental Training Programs and Activities, University of
Georgia, 1992–93

	Number of Programs	Number of Participants
Certified Public Manager	295	8,251
Construction Codes and Energy Conservation	43	1,775
Financial Management	55	1,272
Management Development	282	8,125
Property Tax Assessment and Collection	81	3,268
Other	42	2,060
Total	**798**	**24,751**

Source: 1992-93 Annual Report, Carl Vinson Institute of Government, University of Georgia.

excellent example of what regional universities can accomplish when they invest in a much broader vision of the educational function and mission.

How can universities be encouraged to become more involved in meeting the training and assistance needs of municipalities? How can municipalities be encouraged to take advantage of training modules offered at universities or elsewhere? The task of accomplishing the first two suggestions rests firmly on realizing our last recommendation. That is, the public must come to understand the importance of the investment in training and make decisions based on that importance. It needs to see the connection between the principles and benefits of having "good government" and the actions and results of having a well-trained municipal work force.

Ongoing efforts to educate the public on the importance of the public service abound, especially since the publication of the Volcker Commission's report (National Commission on Public Service, 1989). One such example is found in the Ohio Commission on the Public Service. In its *Final Report and Recommendations,* the commission reasons:

Table 6.3
**Public-Sector Outreach Activities, Bowling Green State University,
1992–93**

	Number of Projects
Economic Development Projects	15
Environmental Projects	7
Financial Projects	5
Personnel Projects	6
Citizen Surveys Projects	5
Management Training and Development Projects	1
Total	**39**

Source: 1992-93 Annual Report, Center for Governmental Research and Public Service, Bowling Green State University.

If the public is to exercise effective oversight of its government, and talented and high-minded individuals are to be attracted to the public service in Ohio, the public image of that sector must change. Efforts should focus on the development of a strong program of civic education for both young people and adult citizens that emphasizes the importance of public service and is designed to develop a balanced and informed view of this vital work. (1993)

As illustrated in Table 6.4, the Ohio Commission on the Public Service offers several recommendations on educating the public about the value of public service.

Municipal officials should not wait for the creation of official commissions before they actively engage in educating the public on the relationship between good government and well-trained employees. In fact, the responsibility to begin this educational process will most likely fall on their shoulders. Within each community, public service education can take place in a variety of settings. It may be incorporated into special school programs and may be the focus of the weekly luncheon speech at the various

Table 6.4
Recommendations for Improving Public Service Education

---

1. The State Board of Education should reexamine the civic education and revise it to include a strong experiential component. This could include such things as:
   a. Community activities appropriate for elementary school children
   b. Public service internships, mentoring, or job-shadowing opportunities for high school students that are structured in a way that both student and agency will take them seriously.
2. Colleges and universities should provide expanded opportunities for students to participate in public service internships of a meaningful nature for which they receive college credits.

Source: Final Report and Recommendations of the Ohio Commission on the Public Service. Ohio General Assembly, May 1993, p. 11. (Above list does not include all of the Commission's recommendations.)

community service organizations. Whatever the forum, public service education should incorporate information about the economics of training and the fact that expenses resulting from badly trained managers and employees far surpass the cost of training programs. The goal is to increase the investment expectations on the part of the citizenry: investments in training and assistance opportunities found at universities and investments in developing greater in-house training capacity at city hall.

A wide variety of training, education, and assistance will be needed by municipalities if they are to confront successfully both current and anticipated challenges. While some cities will need specialized and tailored training and others may require assistance of a more general kind, all local governments will need to learn to respond more proactively to the bureaucratic and policy consequences of increasingly rapid social, cultural, legal, and technological change. Only then will we be assured that local government has the capacity to continue into the twenty-first century its critical mission of being the "instrument of humanity." The process and substance of becoming more proactive to future challenges and crises, however, will certainly require a greater investment and a stronger commitment by all segments of society, especially on the part of the citizens of every community.

Appendix A

Survey Instrument

Name of City

Please rate each of your city government's assistance, training, and information needs in the various areas by using the following scale. The scale ranges from "1" or "least needed" to "5" or "most needed." Use a "0" if the area is not applicable in your city government. Place your rating in the space to the left of each item.

Not Applicable	Least Needed				Most Needed
0	1	2	3	4	5

Rating	*Area*	*Description*
_____	1. Budgeting	Training or assistance in understanding budgetary processes. Budget estimating techniques. Budget formulation and execution. Budgeting for revolving funds, operating funds, capital funds.
_____	2. Program Evaluation/ Needs Assessment	Training or assistance in setting up and implementing studies to evaluate existing programs or to assess community needs for public services. Basic research design. Validity and reliability. Cost-benefit analysis.
_____	3. Equal Employment Opportunity	Training or assistance that focuses on regulations, laws, and court cases pertaining to EEO. Affirmative action issues. Sexual harassment issues.

Rating	Area	Description
_____	4. Contract Management	Training or assistance in negotiating contractual services. How to write mutually beneficial contracts. Measuring contract effectiveness. Managing interlocal contracts.
_____	5. Writing and Oral Communication Skills	Training or assistance designed to enhance writing skills: effective memos and clear reports. Give well-planned, effective oral presentations.
_____	6. Public Works/ Capital Financing	Training or assistance understanding financing for capital needs; e.g., major infrastructure projects.
_____	7. Local Government Data Bank	Access to "raw" data from local governments in your area, including raw data on amounts, sources, and categories of annual revenues and expenditures.
_____	8. Employee Benefits	Training or assistance that develops/enhances necessary skills to administer a variety of employee benefits and service programs. How to select/develop flexible benefits programs or cafeteria plans.
_____	9. Labor Relations	Training or assistance that builds the labor relations skills of the management team. Management's rights and responsibilities, key skills, and techniques–determining negotiability, negotiating labor agreements, preventing unfair labor practices, communicating with labor organizations, resolving grievances, and presenting arbitration cases.
_____	10. Legislative Histories	Access to information about legislative history of programs and laws affecting local government.
_____	11. Personnel Staffing	Training or assistance in the identification and selection of best qualified personnel. Interviewing/advertising techniques.
_____	12. Accounting	Training or assistance in accounting procedures. Bookkeeping, fund accounting, analysis and interpretation of financial statements. Cost accounting, selection procedures for attaining an automated accounting system.
_____	13. Statistical/ Data Analysis	Training or assistance in the use of statistics and quantitative analyses for communicating program results and job performance.
_____	14. Local Government Documents/Reports	Access to documents, government reports, and studies conducted by other municipalities. Examples include other local governments' budgets, master plans, job descriptions, position classifications, contracts, city charters, personnel handbooks, etc.
_____	15. Merit Promotion Principles/Practices	Training or assistance in developing/improving merit systems. Roles and responsibilities of managers, supervisors, and staffing specialists in the merit process.

Rating	Area	Description
_____	16. Disciplinary Practices	Training or assistance that focuses on establishing/maintaining effective disciplinary practices. Counseling techniques. Legal aspects of termination.
_____	17. Safety/Health Conditions	Training or assistance on developing sound practices for occupational safety and health. Quit smoking programs, drug and alcohol abuse counseling. AIDS policies/programs.
_____	18. "How-To/Model" Manuals	Access to manuals/handbooks that provide information on "how-to" conduct a variety of local government activities, including model "classification systems," "master plans," "how-to" manuals on budgeting, etc.
_____	19. Professional Journals and Books	Access to professional journals and books dealing with various aspects of government, law, and public administration.
_____	20. Computer Literacy	Training or assistance in computer concepts, terminology, hardware, and software. Understanding of basic functions of microcomputers. Computer applications in data processing, word processing, office information systems, management information systems, data-based management systems.
_____	21. Cash Management	Training and assistance in effective cash management. How to improve debt collection practices. Payroll record keeping and procedures.
_____	22. Office and Inter-Office Communication and Work Relations	Training or assistance designed to develop skills necessary to improve working relations: the communication process, human relations problems in the workplace, problem-solving techniques, building an effective team environment.
_____	23. Grant Proposal Writing and Administration	Training or assistance in techniques of writing effective grant proposals to public sector and private foundation funding sources. Selection of appropriate fund source. Researching proposal ideas. The grants-process and grantsmanship. Financial aspects of contracts and grants. Reporting requirements.
_____	24. Position Classification/ Wage and Salary Analysis	Training or assistance in arranging positions according to their similarities and differences. Factor Evaluation System. Wage and salary comparisons. Writing position descriptions.
_____	25. Maintenance Functions	Training or assistance in developing maintenance schedules and procedures to prolong capital life.
_____	26. Community Relations	Training or assistance in communicating effectively and positively with the public about city government's policies, programs, and services. Effective interaction with citizens.

Rating	Area	Description
_____	27. Federal/State Government Depository	Access to a federal/state government depository, containing reports, documents, and information about federal and state agencies.
_____	28. Managing Personnel Performance	Training or assistance that focuses on personnel performance and productivity improvements. Development of performance appraisal instruments and performance review techniques. Linking career development opportunities to annual performance review activities.
_____	29. Working with Elected Officials	Training or assistance in working effectively with elected officials. Building consensus with elected officials on establishing realistic goals, objectives, and indicators to measure goal-accomplishment.
_____	30. Census Data	Access to U.S. census data, such as economic and demographic information relevant to the local government and community.

31. Please list other areas in which your organization has a need for training, assistance, or information.

Rating	Area	Description
_____	_____	_____
_____	_____	_____
_____	_____	_____
_____	_____	_____

32. In your opinion, of the areas listed above (items 1-31), which five (5) areas do you think your organization will have the greatest training, assistance, or informational need during the next ten years?

   Item # _____ (Greatest need during next 10 years)

   Item # _____ (2nd greatest need during next 10 years)

   Item # _____ (3rd greatest need during next 10 years)

   Item # _____ (4th greatest need during next 10 years)

   Item # _____ (5th greatest need during next 10 years)

33. What is the total number of full-time professional/administrative (non-clerical) staff in all city departments?

   _____

34. To your knowledge, has your city ever been contacted by a college/university to address your training/assistance/information needs?

        _____ no   _____ yes;   last year contacted: _____ .

35. To your knowledge, has your city ever been contacted by your state's municipal league/local government management association to address your training/assistance/information needs?

        _____ no   _____ yes;   last year contacted: _____ .

36. Distance (in miles) between your city hall and the nearest college or university.

        _____

37. Please list other organizations that have contacted you to address your training/assist-ance/information needs.

Organization	Year last contacted

38. Estimated current population of your city.   _____

Appendix B

Illustrations of Training Modules and Activities

PERSONNEL-RELATED TRAINING MODULES

Americans With Disabilities Act

Purpose: To provide a fundamental knowledge about the Americans with Disabilities Act (ADA).

Goals: Each workshop participant will gain an understanding of three provisions of the ADA: (1) non-discriminatory practices; (2) reasonable-accommodation issues; and (3) undue hardship issues. Workshop participants will also acquire skills in applying the ADA to the specific worksite.

Time: This is a one-day workshop.

Further Information:

The Job Accommodation Network (JAN), 809 Allen Hall, P.O. Box 6122, Morgantown, West Virginia, (800) 526-7234.

Gary S. Marx and Gary G. Goldberger, *Disability Law Compliance Manual* (Boston, Mass.: Warren, Gorham and Lamont, 1991).

Module 1. Overview of the ADA

1. Definitions and coverage
2. What constitutes a disability
3. Substantial limitations on life activities

Module 2. Non-Discriminatory Practices

1. Covered employment actions
2. Specific impairments protected
3. Excluded conditions
4. "Otherwise qualified" provisions
5. "Essential functions" of a job

Module 3. Reasonable-Accommodation Provisions

1. The case-specific nature of reasonable accommodations
2. Notification and documentation of disability
3. Changes in the nature of confidentiality
4. Types of reasonable accommodations
5. "Sufficient" accommodations, compared with the "best" accommodations
6. EEO *Interpretive Guidelines* and congressional intent
7. Costs of reasonable accommodations

Module 4. Undue Hardship

1. What constitutes "undue hardship"
2. Nature and cost of accommodations
3. Characteristics of the facility
4. Characteristics of the entire organization
5. Characteristics of types of operations
6. The relation between reasonable accommodations and undue hardship claims

Managing the Workplace Ramifications of AIDS

Purpose: To prepare management for dealing with workplace situations involving HIV and AIDS.

Goals: By end of training session, participants will have epidemiological, legal, and interpersonal knowledge about HIV and AIDS; and an understanding of how to apply knowledge of HIV / AIDS to their specific work settings.

Time: This is a one-day workshop.

Further Information

James D. Slack. *AIDS and the Public Work Force: Local Government Preparedness in Managing the Epidemic* (Tuscaloosa, Ala.: University of
Alabama Press, 1991).

American Red Cross.

U.S. Centers for Disease Control and Prevention.

James D. Slack and Associates.

Module 1. Understanding HIV and AIDS

The general purpose of Module 1 is to familiarize workshop participants with some of the fears and myths about AIDS that may affect workplace performance; and the experiences of HIV-positive employees, as
they affect workplace performance. Specific topics include:

1. What is HIV and AIDS

2. Modes of transmission

3. Progression from HIV to AIDS

4. AIDS-related diseases

5. Keeping workers healthy and productive

Module 2. Managing the Workplace

The general purpose of Module 2 is to familiarize workshop participants on maintaining a productive and healthy workplace. Topics center
on the Americans with Disabilities Act as it applies to AIDS. Specific topics include:

1. ADA and the specific work setting

2. Non-discrimination of HIV-infected employees

3. Reasonable-accommodation issues and application to specific workplace and job descriptions

4. Undue hardship issues and application to specific workplace and job
descriptions

*Module 3. Dealing Effectively with Both HIV-Positive and
Non-Infected Employees*

Module 3 shifts focus from the "agency" level to the "supervisor-sub-
ordinate" level. Using case law in the areas of labor relations, workforce
management, and AIDS, as well as experiences of HIV-positive employees, this module familiarizes workshop participants with one-to-one situations. Topics include:

1. ADA's requirements of documentation of HIV

2. Sensitivity in dealing with HIV-positive workers

3. ADA's modification of confidentiality

4. Knowledge about community-based assistance programs

5. Controlling rumors, fears, and behavior of employees who are not HIV-positive

Module 4A. Developing an AIDS Plan for the Workplace

Module 4B. Training Staff about AIDS and the Workplace

Workshop participants are divided into two groups. Managers participate in Module 4A, in which the basic components of an AIDS plan for the workplace is discussed. The principles discussed in this chapter are applied to address workplace issues at the specific work setting and at the job-specific level. The purpose of the plan is to maintain a healthy and productive work force while avoiding AIDS-related litigation.

Training staff participate in Module 4B, which focuses on strategies for educating the entire staff on the issue of AIDS. This module includes discussion on presenting AIDS in non-threatening and non-offensive ways, yet in a manner that is direct and provides detailed information. It also focuses on how municipal trainers can tap local expertise and resources, as well as how to disseminate information in an effective manner.

Managerial Styles and Employee Performance

Purpose: To facilitate a better understanding of managerial styles and the relationship between managerial styles and employee performance.

Goals: Workshop participants will develop a clear understanding of (1) theory X and theory Y management; (2) situational management; (3) their own management styles; and (4) how they might deal more effectively with subordinates.

Time: This is a one-day workshop.

Further Information:

James D. Slack and Associates.

Module 1. Managerial Qualities

1. Supervisory attitudes inventory

2. List of qualities admired and disliked

3. Goal-oriented management

Module 2. Theory X and Theory Y

1. Assumptions of both managerial approaches

2. Applications

Module 3. Understanding Yourself

1. Administration of a FIRO-B personality test

2. Discussion of results

Module 4. Application of Managerial Styles to Employee Motivation

1. Based on FIRO-B results, what motivates you

2. Based on FIRO-B results, how you can motivate your employees

Effective Communication Skills

Purpose: To improve oral and written communication skills of first-line managers and above.

Goal: By end of training session, participants will have knowledge about writing effective memos and reports, and giving clear and articulate oral presentations.

Time: This is a four-day workshop.

Further Information:

Rudolph F. Verderber, *The Challenge of Effective Speaking* (Belmont, Calif.: Wadsworth Publishing, 1991).

Day One: Effective Memo and Report Writing

Module 1. Overview of Effective Writing

1. Workshop participants will bring a three-paragraph memo and a five-page report that they have written. Transparencies are made from the memos.

2. Reasons (career, job, personal) for the need for effective writing are reviewed.

Module 2. Components of Effective Memo Writing

1. Developing the purpose statement

2. Getting to the "point": The first sentence/paragraph

3. Reasons for the "point": The second sentence/paragraph

4. Summarizing the "point": The third sentence/paragraph

Module 3. Tips in Effective Memo Writing

1. Writing informative memos
2. Writing persuasive memos
3. Being concise: Cutting down on unnecessary words
4. Being factual: Taking out the emotion
5. Being sure: Putting the memo down and picking it back up
6. Being on time: Getting the memo out

Module 4. Writing Memos

1. Examining memos written: The good, the bad, and the ugly
2. In-class writing of a memo (placed onto transparencies)
3. Examining memos written in class

Day Two: Effective Report Writing

Module 1. Overview of Grammar

1. Writing a sentence
2. Writing a paragraph

Module 2. Components of Effective Reports

1. Executive summaries
2. Purpose and introduction
3. Discussion of methodology
4. Findings
5. Conclusions

Module 3. Tips on Effective Report Writing

1. Being concise
2. Writing the executive summary last
3. Following organization norms and rules

Module 4. Writing Memos and Reports in the Public's Eye

1. The principle of the glass fishbowl
2. Specific legislation governing access

Day Three: Effective Oral Presentations

Module 1. Overview of Public Speaking

1. Fears of speaking publicly
2. Methods of addressing fears

Module 2. Principles of Effective Speaking

1. Understanding audiences
2. Clear-cut goals and purposes
3. Getting information to support goals and purposes
4. Organizing the speech
   - thesis
   - supportive information

Module 3. Tips on Effective Speaking

1. Keeping words simple and avoiding jargon
2. The military way:
   - tell them what you will say
   - say it
   - tell them what you have said
3. Enthusiasm
4. Establishing validity and professionalism
5. Physical presentation
6. Use and non-use of notes
7. Timing and practice

Module 4. The Informative Speech

1. Principles of informative speech
2. Homework assignment: Write a five-minute informative speech

Day Four: Effective Oral Presentation (continued)

Module 1. Practicing Informative Speaking

Each workshop participant gives an informative speech.

Module 2. The Persuasive Speech

1. Principles of persuasive speech
2. Lunch assignment: Transform informative speech into a persuasive speech

Module 3. Practicing Persuasive Speaking

Each workshop participant gives a persuasive speech.

Module 4. The Extemporaneous Speech

1. Principles of extemporaneous speaking

2. Immediate assignment: An extemporaneous speech
Workshop participants are consecutively given a different job-related topic with one minute to prepare a four-minute presentation.

WORKPLACE-OPERATIONS WORKSHOPS

Grant-Writing

Purpose: To familiarize public managers with private foundations and the grant-writing process.

Goals: By the end of the training session, participants will have a clearer understanding of (1) how to search for and select an appropriate funding source; and (2) the process of writing a grant proposal. By the end of the second day, each workshop participant will complete a "polished" rough draft of a proposal.

Time: This is a two-day workshop.

Further Information:

"Program Planning and Proposal Writing" (Los Angeles, Calif.: The Grantsmanship Center, 1980).

Soraya M. Coley and Cynthia A. Scheinberg, *Proposal Writing* (Newbury Park, Calif.: Sage Publications, 1990).

Day One

Module 1. Philosophy of Fund-Raising

1. Know what you want

2. Ask first, before writing a grant proposal

3. Developing community support

4. The homework before submitting a grant proposal

5. The short-term attitude of funding sources

6. Rules for contacting funding source

7. Don't beg

8. Amount of money available through private foundations

9. Rejection

Module 2. Researching Foundations

1. The foundation directory

2. Foundation libraries

3. Annual reports

4. IRS 990–PF forms

Module 3. Step-by-Step Process of Proposal Writing

1. Summary

2. Introduction

3. Problem statement/needs assessment

4. Objectives

5. Methods

6. Evaluation

7. Budget

8. Future

9. Appendix

Day Two

Each participant begins to write a grant. The workshop facilitator assists and answers questions.

Public Works/Capital Finance

Purpose: To provide expertise in "construction inspection" techniques.
Goal: Each workshop participant will obtain hands-on information on the inspection of above- and sub-ground public works. A certificate is awarded to participants who successfully complete the workshop.
Time: This is a two-day workshop.

Further Information:

American Public Works Association, 1313 E. 60th Street, Chicago, Illinois 60637.

Day One

Module 1. Contract Documents

1. Contract documents

2. General provisions

3. Technical provisions

4. Review, examination, and discussion

Module 2. Inspection Duties and Records

1. The inspector
2. Inspection duties
3. Inspection records
4. Review, examination, and discussion

Module 3. Underground Pipeline Construction

1. Basics of pipeline systems
2. Installation of pipeline systems
3. Problems encountered during construction
4. Review, examination, and discussion

Day Two

Module 1. Embankments, Subgrades, and Foundations

1. Soil fundamentals
2. Soil compaction, embankment, and subgrade basics
3. Embankment and subgrade construction and control
4. Review, examination, and discussion

Module 2. Concrete Construction

1. Raw materials, concrete mix design
2. Concrete construction and preparation
3. Concrete construction and placement
4. Review, examination, and discussion

Module 3. Asphaltic Concrete Construction

1. Raw materials, asphaltic concrete mixes
2. Asphaltic concrete construction and preparation
3. Asphaltic concrete construction and placement
4. Review, examination, and discussion

PROGRAM-RELATED WORKSHOPS

Program Evaluation

Purpose: To familiarize participants with the concepts and steps involved
   in conducting and presenting a program evaluation.

Goals: Workshop participants will have a firm understanding of the scientific method, issues pertaining to measurement and data collection, and appropriate types of statistics. They will also learn to use tables and graphs in the presentation of results.

Time: This is a two-day workshop.

Further Information:

Delbert C. Miller, *Handbook of Research Design and Social Measurement* (Newbury Park, Calif.: Sage, 1991).

Lynn Lyons Morris and Carol Taylor Fitz-Gibbon, *How to Present an Evaluation Report* (Beverly Hills, Calif.: Sage, 1978).

Elizabethann O'Sullivan and Gary R. Rassel, *Research Methods for Public Administrators* (White Plains, N.Y.: Longman, 1988).

Day One

Module 1. Research Designs

1. Experimental designs
2. Quasi-experimental designs
3. Pre-experimental designs
4. Internal validity
5. External validity

Module 2. Measurement

1. Levels of measurement
2. Validity of measurement
3. Reliability of measurement

Module 3. Data Collection

1. Citizen surveys
2. Collecting office data
3. Secondary data
4. Academic information sources

Day Two

Module 4. Statistics

1. Univariate and contingency table analysis
2. Regression analysis and correlation

Module 5. Presenting Evaluation Reports

1. Front cover

2. Summary statement

3. Background information

4. Description of project

5. Reporting the results

6. Discussion of the results

7. Costs and benefits

Neighborhood Block Analysis

Purpose: To train municipal employees on preparing, conducting and utilizing the results of ε neighborhood block analysis.

Goals: Workshop participants will learn to assess basic, observable neighborhood conditions, including
   - exterior housing conditions
   - street and drainage conditions
   - land and building vacancies
   - safety hazards
   - other items and concerns of the city

Time: This is a one-day training session. Implementation time is a function of the number of blocks in the community.

Further Information:

James D. Slack and Associates.

Methodology

The neighborhood block survey is a methodology developed by the Texas Department of Health in the 1950s. The survey is accomplished by teams, which ideally consist of a driver, an observer, and a recorder. Each team should be responsible for no more than twenty-five city blocks. This methodology entails several steps.

Step 1. Training Workshop

Each team is given the necessary materials in one packet and the methodology is reviewed. A slide show is presented to provide examples and typical situations.

Step 2. Pre-test

Upon completion of the workshop, each team conducts a trial survey of five identical blocks. The teams return to the workshop and the block maps are examined and compared. This step is to ensure reliability.

Step 3. Block Survey

Upon completion of the pre-test, teams drive to assigned sections of the community. Each team begins at the northwest corner of each designated block, drives once around the block to review the general environmental conditions, and then drives around the same block a second time to observe and record the location of specific conditions. The team then proceeds to the next block and repeats the process. The driver of each team should not exceed five miles per hour but should never drive under two miles per hour. At no time should the car come to a complete stop.

Step 4. Data Tabulation

Upon completion of the block survey, teams record the data from each block map on tabulation sheets.

Step 5. Color-Coding City Maps

For each factor, such as housing, safety, or street conditions, a large city map is coded by color to indicate variations in block conditions. To illustrate: if a block has only sound houses, it is colored in blue; if a block has sound and deteriorating houses, it is colored in green; if a block has dilapidated houses but fewer dilapidated than deteriorating or sound houses, it is colored in yellow; if the majority of houses on the block are dilapidated, that block is colored in red.

Another large city map is coded according to the next factor, such as safety hazards. Here it does not matter whether a block has one or fifty safety hazards; each block with a safety hazard is colored in red. Another large city map is coded according to each factor, such as street conditions. Here, each pothole is coded in red at its approximate location on the map.

This process permits city officials to see general situations on the large city maps and then to consult the individual block map (such as in the case of a safety hazard) to pinpoint the specific condition and its location.

Step 6. Computer Analysis

Measures of association are utilized to analyze data from the tabulation sheets.

EXTERNAL-RELATIONS WORKSHOPS

Working with the Media

Purpose: To prepare managers to work effectively with members of the local media.

Goals: Workshop participants will learn to conduct and control press conferences, interview situations, and control the image of the organization.

Time: This is a two-day workshop.

Further Information:

Public Works Management Program, College of Urban Affairs, Cleveland State University, Cleveland, Ohio 44115.

Day One

Module 1. Local Government and the Media

1. Overview of the local media
2. How the media operate
3. What they want
4. What makes a story
5. Type of interviews
   - Feature/profile
   - Hard news
   - Issues
   - Hostile/Investigative

Module 2. Videotape Scenario 1 (Hostile)

Distribute scenario description to all participants. Trainer poses as investigative TV reporter with camera crew, conducts five-minute "ambush" interviews in "building lobby" with each participant, in front of entire group, varying questions for each participant.

Module 3. Identifying Your Key Points

1. What issues are facing you?
2. What's your message?
3. How to get your message across
4. Conveying your points in a news release

Module 4. Critique of Scenario 1 Interviews

Module 5. Videotape Scenario 2 (Hard News)

Trainer poses as radio reporter, conducts five-minute "phone" interviews with each participant in front of entire group, based on participants' press releases.

Module 6. Critique of Scenario 2 Interviews

Module 7. Press Release

Each participant writes a press release, which is then evaluated.

Day Two

Module 1. Videotape Scenario 3 (Feature/Profile)

Trainer poses as TV talk show host, conducts five- to seven-minute interviews with each participant based on individual background information provided by each participant in advance. Interviews are conducted in front of the group.

Module 2. Critique of Scenario 3

Module 3. News Conference

Workshop group prepares a "news conference" based on Scenario 1, appointing one participant as group spokesperson. News conference is videotaped.

Module 4. Critique of Videotape

Module 5. Working with the Media

1. Developing relationships
2. How to make enemies
3. What to do when they call

Module 6. Preparing for the Interview

1. Questions to ask
2. The interview site
3. What to wear
4. Rehearsal

Module 7. Image

1. Body language and eye contact
2. Gestures
3. Posture

4. Voice

Module 8. Videotape Scenario 4 (Issues)

Trainer posing as TV reporter conducts five-minute interviews with each participant in his or her "office" with camera crew shooting footage. Each participant is interviewed in front of the group using varying questions.

Module 9. Critique of Scenario 4 — Interviews

Public Leadership Training

Purpose: To help local government leaders mobilize their resources, develop skills, and create the environment essential for collaborative problem-solving.

Goals: An assessment center methodology is used. Twelve participants complete eight activities over a two-day period. Expert observers work together to reach a consensus on the final composite evaluation ratings for each participant, then provide confidential feedback to the participants related to the dimensions of successful public leadership. Suggestions for individualized personal development plans are provided upon request.

Time: This is a two-day workshop.

Further Information:

David M. Boothe, Project EXCEL, OSU/OCES Center, P.O. Box 958, Jackson, Ohio 45640, (614) 286-3299.

Day One

Twelve participants take part in eight individual and group activities designed specifically for their public positions. Activities include:

- Group discussion A
- Group discussion B
- Fact finding
- Media discussion
- In-basket exercise
- Background interview
- Case study activity
- Interview simulation

The eight activities give assessors the opportunity to observe participants' strengths in each of fifteen dimensions of public leadership:

- Leadership
- Oral communications
- Initiative
- Behavioral flexibility
- Sensitivity
- Planning and organizing
- Assertiveness
- Collaborativeness
- Objectivity
- Decision-making/judgment
- Perception
- Management control
- Written communication
- Organization sensitivity
- Development of co-workers

Day Two

The assessors reach consensus on the participants' observed strengths and weaknesses in the fifteen dimensions. They provide confidential feedback and suggestions for professional development plans.

Municipal Officials and the U.S.-Mexican Border

Purpose: To provide public managers with a better understanding of opportunities and challenges along the U.S.-Mexican border.

Goals: Using a lecture-discussion format, participants will learn about economic, political, and social issues confronting both sides of the border.

Time: This is a one-day workshop.

Further Information:

Department of Public Policy and Administration, California State University, Bakersfield.

Module 1. Historical Overview of the Border

Module 2. Border Demography

Module 3. The Mexican Political System and Culture

Module 4. The North American Free Trade Agreement

Module 5. Economic Opportunities and Challenges
Module 6. Health Care Opportunities and Challenges
Module 7. Education Opportunities and Challenges
Module 8. Local Government Opportunities and Challenges

References

Abney, G., and T. P. Lauth. 1986. *The Politics of State and City Administration*. Albany, N.Y.: State University of New York Press.

Accordino, J. J. 1989. "Quality-of-Working-Life Systems in Large Cities: An Assessment." *Public Productivity Review* 12(4): 345–60.

Ammons, D. N., and J. J. Glass. May/June 1988. "Headhunters in Local Government: Use of Executive Search Firms in Managerial Selection." *Public Administration Review* 48: 687–93.

Bailey, Thomas. Spring 1990. "Jobs of the Future and the Skills They Will Require." *American Educator*: 10–16, 40–44.

Ban, Carolyn, Sue R. Faerman, and Norma M. Riccucci. 1992. "Productivity and the Personnel Process." In Marc Holzer, ed., *Public Productivity Handbook*, 401–23. New York: Marcel Dekker.

Bandura, Albert. 1977a. "Self-Efficacy: Toward a Unifying Theory of Behavioral Change." *Psychological Review* 84: 191–215.

———. 1977b. *Social Learning Theory*. Englewood Cliffs, N.J.: Prentice-Hall.

Banovitz, James M., ed. 1984. *Small Cities and Counties: A Guide to Managing Services*. Washington, D.C.: International City Management Association.

Berman, David. 1992. "State-Local Relations: Mandates, Money, Partnerships." In *ICMA the Municipal Year Book 1992*, 51–55. Washington, D.C.: International City Management Association.

Bernold, Thomas, and James Finkelstein. 1987. *Computer Assisted Approaches to Training: Foundations of Industry's Future*. Amsterdam, Netherlands: Elsevier Science Publishers B.V.

Berryman-Fink, Cynthia. 1985. "Male and Female Managers' Views of the Communication Skills and Training Needs of Women in Management." *Public Personnel Management* 14(3): 307–13.

Bishop, Peter C., and Augustus J. Jones, Jr. March/April 1993. "Implementing the Americans with Disabilities Act of 1990: Assessing the Variables of Success." *Public Administration Review* 53(2): 121–28.

Blease Graham, Cole, Jr. 1990. "Equal Employment Opportunity and Affirmative Action." In Steven Hayes and Richard Kearney, eds., *Public Personnel Administration*, 2nd edn., 177–93. Englewood Cliffs, N.J.: Prentice-Hall.

Bozeman, Barry, and Dianne Rahm. 1989. "The Explosion of Technology." In James L. Perry, ed., *Handbook of Public Administration*, 54–67. San Francisco: Jossey-Bass Publishers.

Brown, Anthony. January/February 1980. "Technical Assistance to Rural Communities: Stopgap or Capacity Building?" *Public Administration Review* 40: 18–23.

Bullard, Angela M., and Deil S. Wright. May/June 1993. "Circumventing the Glass Ceiling: Women Executives in American State Governments." *Public Administration Review* 53(3): 189–202.

Campbell, John P. 1988. "Training Design for Performance Improvement." In John P. Campbell, Richard J. Campbell and Associates, *Productivity in Organizations: New Perspectives from Industrial and Organizational Psychology*, 177–215. San Francisco: Jossey-Bass Publishers.

Carper, Donald, et al. 1991. *Understanding the Law*. St. Paul, Minn.: West Publishing Co.

Carr, Adam F. 1988. "Utility Analysis and Human Resources Management." *Public Productivity Review* 12(2): 131–47.

Cascio, Wayne F. 1989. "Using Utility Analysis to Assess Training Outcomes." In Irwin L. Goldstein and Associates. *Training and Development in Organizations*, 63–88. San Francisco: Jossey-Bass Publishers.

Cassner-Lotto, Jill, and Associates. 1988. *Successful Training Strategies: Twenty-six Innovative Corporate Models*. San Francisco: Jossey-Bass Publishers.

Cigler, Beverly A. 1990. "County Contracting: Reconciling the Accountability and Information Paradoxes." Symposium on "Rural Public Administration and Public Policy." James D. Slack, symposium ed., *Public Administration Quarterly* 14(3): 285–301.

———. January 1987. "Building a Database: The 'National' Small Government Research Network." *New Directions in Public Administration Research* 1: 110–28.

————. November–December 1984. "Small City and Rural Governance: The Changing Environment." *Public Administration Review* 44: 540–45.

Congressional Record, S10735, September 7, 1989.

Craig, Robert. 1987. *Training and Development Handbook,* 3rd edn. New York: McGraw-Hill Book Co.

Crapo, Raymond F. 1986. "It's Time to Stop Training . . . and Start Facilitating." *Public Personnel Management* 15(4): 443–49.

Davis, Charles, and Jonathan West. Summer 1984. "Implementing Public Programs: Equal Employment Opportunity, Affirmative Action, and Administrative Policy Options." *Review of Public Personnel Administration* 4(3): 16–30.

DeSario, Jack, et al. 1991. "Management of Human Resources in Local Government." In Richard Bingham, *Managing Local Government.* Newbury Park, Calif.: Sage Publications.

Dillman, Don A., and Kenneth R. Tremblay, Jr. January 1977. "The Quality of Life in Rural America." *Annals of the American Academy of Political and Social Sciences* 49: 115–29.

Dometrius, Nelson, and Lee Sigelman. May–June 1984. "Assessing Programs Toward Affirmative Action Goals in State and Local Government." *Public Administration Review* 44(3): 241–46.

Dunn, Delmer D., Frank K. Gibson, and Joseph Whorton, Jr. July–August 1985. "University Commitment to Public Service for State and Local Governments." *Public Administration Review* 45: 503–9.

Elazar, Daniel. 1984. *American Federalism: A View from the States,* 3rd edn. New York: Harper and Row.

Eurich, Nell P. 1985. *Corporate Classrooms: The Learning Business.* Princeton, N.J.: Carnegie Foundation for the Advancement of Teaching.

Faerman, Sue R., and Carolyn Ban. 1993. "Trainee Satisfaction and Training Impact: Issues in Training Evaluation." *Public Productivity and Management Review* 16(3): 299–314.

Faerman, Sue R., and Theodore D. Peters. 1991. "A Conceptual Framework for Examining Managerial Roles and Transitions Across Levels of Organizational Hierarchy." *Proceedings of the National Public Management Research Conference,* 112–23.

Fisher, Cynthia D. 1989. "Current and Recurrent Challenges in HRM." *Journal of Management* 15(2): 157–80.

Flanders, Loretta. 1989. "Developing Executive and Managerial Talent." In James L. Perry, ed., *Handbook of Public Administration,* 424–36. San Francisco: Jossey-Bass Publishers.

Florestano, Patricia S., and Stephen B. Gordon. January–February 1980. "Public vs. Private: Small Government Contracting with the Private Sector." *Public Administration Review* 40: 444–53.

Forrester, Jay W. 1965. "A New Corporate Design." *Industrial Management Review* 7(1): 5–17.

Gabris, G. T. 1989. "Implementing More Productive Management Training Programs." *Public Productivity Review* 12(4): 437–44.

Glenn-Ryan, Rebecca, and Edward Guss. Winter 1989. "Training and Organizational Change." *Public Productivity and Management Review* 13(2): 187–93.

Gold, Steven, and Brenda Erickson. Winter 1989. "State Aid to Local Governments in the 1980s." *State and Local Government Review* 21: 11–22.

Goldstein, Gerald S., and Ronald G. Ehrenberg. July 1976. "Executive Compensation in Municipalities." *Southern Economic Journal* 43: 937–47.

Goldstein, Irwin L. 1986. *Training in Organizations: Needs Assessment, Development and Evaluation,* 2nd edn. Pacific Grove, Calif.: Brooks Cole Publishing Co.

Gordon, George. 1992. *Public Administration in America,* 4th edn. New York: St. Martin's Press.

Gudykunst, William B. 1991. *Bridging Differences: Effective Intergroup Communication.* Newbury Park, Calif.: Sage Publications.

Haas, Peter. Summer 1991. "A Comparison of Training Priorities of Local Government Employees and Their Supervisors." *Public Personnel Management* 20(2): 225–32.

Hambrick, Ralph. Winter 1983. "University-Based Professional Service as a Question of Organization Design." *State and Local Government Review* 21: 11–22.

Hiatt, Robert A., Bruce Fireman, Charles P. Quesenberry, Jr., and Joseph V. Selby. 1988. "The Impact of AIDS on the Kaiser Permanente Medical Care Program (Northern California Region)." Prepared for the Health Program, Office of Technology Assessment, U.S. Congress, Washington, D.C.

Hood, Christopher C. 1986. *The Tools of Government.* Chatham, N.J.: Chatham House Publishers.

Hudson Institute. 1988. *Civil Service 2000.* Washington, D.C.: U.S. Office of Personnel Management.

Hussey, David E. 1990. "Management Strategy and Corporate Strategy." In David E. Hussey and Phil Lowe, eds., *Key Issues in Management Training,* 5–8. London: Kogan Page Ltd.

Hyde, Albert, and Jay Shafritz. 1989. "Training and Development and Personnel Management." In International Personnel Management Association, *Reading on Perspectives in Training.* Alexandria, Va.: International Personnel Management Association.

International City Management Association. 1988. *The Municipal Yearbook*. Washington, D.C.: ICMA.

International Personnel Management Association. 1992. *1992 Public Personnel Inventory*. Alexandria, Va.: International Personnel Management Association.

Job Accommodation Network. 809 Allen Hall, P.O. Box 6122, Morgantown, W.Va. 26507-9984; phone: (800) 526-7234.

Johnson, James A., and Walter J. Jones. September–October 1991. "AIDS: Perspectives on Public Health, Policy, and Administration." *Public Administration Review* 51: 456–60.

Katz, Sally N., and Leslie S. Rosen. 1987. "Management Training for a Technical Population." *Training and Development Journal* 41(10): 71–73.

Kirkpatrick, Donald L. 1987. "Evaluation." In Robert L. Craig, ed., *Training and Development Handbook*, 3rd edn., 301–19. New York: McGraw-Hill Book Co.

Knowles, Malcolm S. 1987. "Adult Learning." In Robert L. Craig, ed., *Training and Development Handbook*, 3rd edn., 168–79. New York: McGraw-Hill Book Co.

Lan, Zhiyong, and David H. Rosenbloom. November–December 1992. "Public Administration in Transition?" *Public Administration Review* 52(6): 537–47.

Latham, Gary P. 1989. "Behavioral Approaches to the Training Process." In Irwin L. Goldstein and Associates, *Training and Development in Organizations*, 256–95. San Francisco: Jossey-Bass Publishers.

———. 1988. "Human Resource Training and Development." *Annual Review of Psychology* 39: 545–82.

Lewis, J. R., and J. R. Raffel. 1988. "Training Public Administrators to Work with Legislators." *Public Productivity Review* 11(4): 101–8.

Lineberry, Robert, and Edmund Fowler. September 1967. "Reformism and Public Policies in American Cities." *American Political Science Review* 61: 705–25.

London, Manuel, and Richard A. Wueste. 1992. *Human Resource Development in Changing Organizations*. Westport, Conn.: Quorum Books.

McGehee, William, and Paul W. Thayer. 1961. *Training in Business and Industry*, New York: John Wiley & Sons.

MacManus, S. A., and W. J. Pammer, Jr. 1990. "Cutbacks in the County: Retrenchment in Rural Villages, Townships and Counties." Symposium on "Rural Public Administration and Public Policy," James D. Slack, symposium ed. *Public Administration Quarterly* 14(3): 302–23.

Miller, Kathleen D. 1989. *Retraining the American Workforce*. Reading, Mass.: Addison-Wesley Publishing Co.

Morgan, David. 1989. *Managing Urban Government*. Pacific Grove, Calif.: Brooks/Cole Publishing.

Morgan, David R., and John Pelissero. December 1980. "Urban Policy: Does Political Structure Matter?" *American Political Science Review* 75: 999–1006.

Mosher, Frederick C. 1968. *Democracy and the Public Service*. New York: Oxford University Press.

National Commission on the Public Service. 1989. *Report of the National Commission on Public Service*. Washington, D.C.: U.S. Government Printing Office.

Nelles, H. V. 1990. "Red Tied: Fin de Siecle Politics in Ontario." In Michael Whittington and Glen Williams, eds., *Canadian Politics in the 1990s*, 76–97. Scarborough, Ontario: Nelson Publishers.

Neugarten, Dail. 1990. "Sexual Harassment in Public Employment." In Steven Hayes and Richard Kearney, eds., *Public Personnel Administration*, 205–14. Englewood Cliffs, N.J.: Prentice-Hall.

Newell, Terry. 1989. "The Future and Federal Training." In International Personnel Management Association, *Readings on Perspectives in Training*, 15–28. Alexandria, Va.: International Personnel Management Association.

Newstrom, John W. 1986. "Leveraging Management Development through the Management of Transfer." *Journal of Management Development* 5(5): 33–45.

Office of Technology Assessment. 1986. *Technology and Structural Unemployment: Reemploying Displaced Adults*. OTA No:052–003–01017–8. Washington, D.C.: U.S. Government Printing Office.

Ohio Public Service Commission. May 1993. "Preparing State and Local Government for the 21st Century." *Final Report and Recommendations of the Ohio Commission on the Public Service*. Ohio General Assembly.

Ostroff, Cheri, and J. Kevin Ford. 1989. "Assessing Training Needs: Critical Levels of Analysis." In Irwin L. Goldstein and Associates, *Training and Development in Organizations*, 25–62. San Francisco: Jossey-Bass Publishers.

Pammer, William. 1992. "The Future of Municipal Finances in an Era of Fiscal Austerity and Economic Globalization." In *ICMA The Municipal Yearbook 1992*. Washington, D.C.: International City Management Association.

Patterson, Thomas. 1993. *The American Democracy*, 2nd edn. New York: McGraw-Hill.

Pohlmann, Marcus D. 1993. *Governing the Postindustrial City*. New York: Longman.

Poister, T. H., and G. Streib. May–June 1989a. "Management Tools in Municipal Government: Trends Over the Past Decade." *Public Administration Review* 49: 240–48.

———. 1989b. "Municipal Managers' Concerns for Productivity Improvement." *Public Productivity and Management Review* 13(1): 3–12.

Rehfuss, John. 1989. *The Job of Public Manager*. Chicago: Dorsey Press.

Report of the Task Force on Education and Training to the National Commission on the Public Service. 1989. "Investment for Leadership: Education and Training for the Public Service." In *Task Force Reports to the National Commission on the Public Service*, 113–55. Washington, D.C.: National Commission on the Public Service.

Robinson, Dana Gaines, and James C. Robinson. 1989. *Training for Impact: How to Link Training to Business Needs and Measure the Results*. San Francisco: Jossey-Bass Publishers.

Rubin, Irene S. January–February 1988. "Municipal Enterprises: Exploring Budgetary and Political Implications." *Public Administration Review* 48: 542–50.

Schmidt, Frank L., John E. Hunter, and Kenneth Pearlman. 1982. "Assessing the Economic Impact of Personnel Programs on Workforce Productivity." *Personnel Psychology* 35: 333–47.

Sherwood, Frank P. 1983. "The Education and Training of Public Managers." In William B. Eddy, ed., *Handbook of Organization Management*, 43–68. New York: Marcel Dekker.

Slack, James D. 1991. *AIDS and the Public Work Force: Local Government Preparedness in Managing the Epidemic*. Tuscaloosa, Ala.: University of Alabama Press.

———. 1990. "Local Government Training and Education Needs for the Twenty-First Century." *Public Productivity and Management Review* 13(4): 397–404.

Slack, James, and Lee Sigelman. December 1987. "City Managers and Affirmative Action: Testing a Model of Linkage." *Western Political Quarterly* 40(4): 673–84.

Sokolow, Alvin D., and Beth Walter Hondale. September–October 1984. "How Rural Local Governments Budget: The Alternatives to Executive Preparation." *Public Administration Review* 44: 373–83.

Sterns, Harvey L., and Dennis Doverspike. 1989. "Aging and the Training and Learning Process." In Irwin L. Goldstein and Associates, *Training and Development in Organizations*, 299–332. San Francisco: Jossey-Bass Publishers.

Thai, Khi V., and David Sullivan. January–February 1989. "Impact of Termination of General Revenue Sharing on New England Local Government Finance." *Public Administration Review* 49: 61–67.

Timpone, Joseph, and Paul Sussman. Spring 1988. "Excellence Training for Productivity." *Public Productivity Review* 11(3): 105–15.

Tucker, Florence D. 1985. "A Study of the Training Needs of Older Workers: Implications for Human Resources Development Planning." *Public Personnel Management* 14(1): 85–95.

U.S. Advisory Commission on Intergovernmental Relations. 1992. *Significant Features of Fiscal Federalism*, vol. 2. Washington, D.C.: U.S. Advisory Commission on Intergovernmental Relations.

U.S. Bureau of the Census. 1991. *Public Employment 1990*. Washington, D.C.: U.S. Government Printing Office.

U.S. Department of Health and Human Services, Public Health Service, Centers for Disease Control, Center for Infectious Disease, Division of HIV / AIDS. July 1993. *HIV/AIDS Surveillance Report*. Washington, D.C.: U.S. Department of Health and Human Services.

————. January 1992. *HIV/AIDS Surveillance Report*. Washington, D.C.: U.S. Department of Health and Human Services.

U.S. Department of Health and Human Services, Public Health Service, Centers for Disease Control, Office of the Deputy Director (HIV). February 1991. *CDC HIV/AIDS Prevention*, p. 3. Washington, D.C.: U.S. Department of Health and Human Services.

U.S. General Accounting Office. September 1989. *Senior Executive Service: Training and Development of Senior Executives*, GAO/GGD–89–127. Washington, D.C.: U.S. General Accounting Office.

Van Wart, Montgomery, N. Joseph Cayer, and Steve Cook. 1993. *Handbook of Training and Development for the Public Sector*. San Francisco: Jossey-Bass Publishers.

Weinberg, Mark. Fall 1984. "Budget Retrenchment in Small Cities: A Comparative Analysis of Wooster and Athens, Ohio." *Public Budgeting and Finance* 4: 46–57.

Wexley, Kenneth N. 1984. "Personnel Training." *Annual Review of Psychology* 35: 519–51.

Wexley, Kenneth, and Gary Latham. 1991. *Developing and Training Human Resources in Organizations*, 2nd edn. New York: HarperCollins Publishers.

Whorton, Joseph W., Jr., Frank K. Gibson, and Delmer D. Dunn. January–February 1986. "The Culture of University of Public Service: A National Survey of the Perspectives of Users and Providers." *Public Administration Review* 46: 38–49.

Wilson, Woodrow. May–June 1984. "The New Meaning of Government." *Public Administration Review* 44(3): 193–95. (Originally printed in *Women's Home Companion* 39(11), November 1912.)

Wiseman, M. 1989. "Resistance to Training." *Public Productivity and Management Review* 13(1): 89–98.

Wooldridge, Blue. Winter 1988. "Increasing the Productivity of Public Sector Training." *Public Productivity Review* 12(2): 205–17.

Wright, Deil. 1988. *Understanding Intergovernmental Relations*, 3rd edn. Pacific Grove, Calif.: Brooks/Cole.

Zar, Carol, and Tomasina Stephon. 1991. "Using the Action Research Model to Discover Developmental Needs of Local Government Officials." Unpublished manuscript.

COURT CASES

Griggs v. Duke Power Company. 1971. 401 U.S. 424.

Johnson v. Transportation Agency, Santa Clara County. 1987. 480 U.S. 616.

Local 28 of the Sheetmetal Workers International v. EEOC. 1986. 478 U.S. 421.

Regents of University of California v. Bakke. 1978. 438 U.S. 265.

U.S. v. Paradise. 1987. 480 U.S. 149.

Index

About the Authors

JACK P. DeSARIO is Associate Professor at Mount Union College and director of the pre-law program. Chair of the Ohio Ethic Commission, he publishes extensively in areas of public policy. Among his books are *Citizen Participation and Democracy* (Greenwood, 1987) and *Managing Local Government*.

SUE R. FAERMAN is Associate Professor in the Department of Public Administration, State University of New York at Albany. She publishes in the areas of management education and development and managerial transitions, and is co-author of *Becoming a Master Manager*.

JAMES D. SLACK is Associate Professor in the Department of Public Policy and Administration, California State University at Bakersfield. He is recipient of the Burchfield Award in public administration for his research on the public administration of AIDS. Among his publications are *AIDS and the Public Work Force: Local Government Preparedness in Managing the Epidemic* and *Managing Local Government*.

ISBN 0-89930-697-7

90000>

EAN

9 780899 306971

HARDCOVER BAR CODE